What people

Beyond

Dr Vardy's book is a bracing tonic. When a culture ceases to focus on truth above all other concerns, it becomes a slum peopled by self-serving ideologues, ever in danger of imploding into insanity and increasing silliness. This book offers a diagnosis on many fronts and offers a therapy, from sources old and new, to cure what ails us. For him 'post truth' must lead to a new getting of wisdom. This book will be a valuable resource for educators, their directors and their students, and a sign of hope for us all.
Professor Anthony Kelly CssR

In a post-truth world, this is a splendidly energetic and thoughtful book about discovery and truth. The great questions of our destiny and of what it means to be human are often ignored on the one hand by the relativists who believe that 'my truth' is what matters, and on the other hand by fundamentalists who wish to impose their 'truth' on the world. The critique of modern educational aims is especially telling.
Christopher Lewis, Christ's College, Oxford

In this lucid and comprehensive study, Peter Vardy challenges contemporary relativism, nihilism, and anti-realism. Aflame with passion, he makes a strong case and champions the age-old quest of truth-seeking. He argues that the voice of the Eternal has been largely silenced by post-truth culture—in this book he seeks to reawaken our consciousness.
Professor Dan Cohn-Sherbok

I absolutely loved this book. Peter Vardy surveys 2500 years of philosophical thought, and brings the wisdom of the centuries to bear on our shallow post-truth society. Vardy argues cogently for values that are thoughtlessly swept aside in a relativistic culture. His book should be compulsory reading for all who teach Religious Studies and Philosophy, their pupils and society.

Sarah McDonald, Head of Philosophy and Religion, Haileybury College

Peter Vardy is a brilliant teacher and has produced here an invigorating alternative to prevailing ideas. *Beyond The Cave* provides a vital resource which invites us to fully consider what is at stake in the pursuit of truth. This book will inspire a new wave of enquiry into the nature of truth, what it means to be human and why all this matters.

Kate Rogers, Head of Religion and Philosophy, Chiswick School

A wonderfully written book. All students should be encouraged to ready this as it provides an opportunity to think deeply and to be challenged about the Nature of Truth and what it means to be human free from the cultural obsession with materialism.

Margaret Daniels, Head of Religious Studies, Queen Mary's High School, Walsall.

Beyond The Cave

A philosopher's quest for Truth

Beyond The Cave

A philosopher's quest for Truth

Peter Vardy

IFF
BOOKS

Winchester, UK
Washington, USA

JOHN HUNT PUBLISHING

First published by iff Books, 2020
iff Books is an imprint of John Hunt Publishing Ltd., No. 3 East Street, Alresford,
Hampshire SO24 9EE, UK
office@jhpbooks.com
www.johnhuntpublishing.com
www.iff-books.com

For distributor details and how to order please visit the 'Ordering' section on our website.

Text copyright: Peter Vardy 2018

ISBN: 978 1 78904 174 3
978 1 78904 175 0 (ebook)
Library of Congress Control Number: 2018952786

All rights reserved. Except for brief quotations in critical articles or reviews, no part of this
book may be reproduced in any manner without prior written permission from the publishers.

The rights of Peter Vardy as author have been asserted in accordance with the Copyright,
Designs and Patents Act 1988.

A CIP catalogue record for this book is available from the British Library.

Design: Stuart Davies

UK: Printed and bound by CPI Group (UK) Ltd, Croydon, CR0 4YY
US: Printed and bound by Thomson-Shore, 7300 West Joy Road, Dexter, MI 48130

We operate a distinctive and ethical publishing philosophy in
all areas of our business, from our global network of authors to
production and worldwide distribution.

Contents

This book is dedicated to the founding members of the London Society for the Study of Religions – see Epilogue.

Part One

The Descent Into The Cave

Chapter One

The Beginnings of the Quest

Two dragons stand on either side of us:

1. POSTMODERNISM AND RELATIVISM – these represent a denial of any single truth. We are told that we construct meaning and that it depends on culture, gender, sexuality and other factors. We are in water world, adrift on a sea of flux with no anchor points. Tolerance is the new god and any position must be respected as the days of absolutes are past. Any claim to absolute Truth that is seen to be intolerant of other alternatives is arrogant and discriminatory and all positions are equally legitimate. We are in a post-truth world.
2. FUNDAMENTALISM – this claims to know the truth and seeks to impose its certainties on others. Fundamentalists are increasingly common in some forms of religious education round the world and are growing in influence in institutional religion as well as among atheists.

Between these two dragons runs a shy and retiring little stream. This stream is the search for Truth (the capital 'T' is significant). The stream often appears cowed by the power of the dragons; it is seen as insignificant and unimportant as well as being disregarded by many – as is the way with streams. Nevertheless, a feature of streams is that they cannot be destroyed and beneath the power and seeming dominance of the modern age is the still small voice that calls us to a search for Truth.

Seemingly we live in a post-truth world. In 2016 Oxford Dictionaries declared 'post-truth' to be the word of the year. 'Alternative facts' are meant to be taken as seriously as reporting by reliable media outlets backed up by strong evidence. 'Expert opinion' is widely decried. How has this come about? The aim of this book is to explore the issue of the decline of Truth but do so within a broader context and agenda which will mean addressing questions about what it means to be human as well as the developing role of artificial intelligence and the relevance, or possibly lack of it, of religion. It will also mean addressing the question of human potential and whether there are any transcendent, Eternal and enduring values that may be worth living, and possibly dying, for.

The very idea of Eternal values has today largely been marginalised for reasons that this book will explore. This marginalisation has certainly been aided by the decline in institutional religion in the Western world. Nevertheless, the process has been rendered much easier by the development of anthropology, psychology and sociology which have presented reductionist explanations of the religious impulse and, in so doing, have convincingly portrayed it in ways which render the idea of the Eternal largely redundant. Philosophy should have championed the search for Truth but it, particularly in the Anglo-American tradition, has become increasingly preoccupied with linguistic analysis. The relevance of a subject such as metaphysics has become marginalised or ignored.

Why does the concept of Eternal or transcendent values matter in a supposedly post-truth world? There are various reasons:

1. It affirms the idea of absolute Truth which the post-truth world rejects.
2. It stands for a meaning and purpose for human existence that is not simply constructed or the result of social convention.
3. It can represent an ontological distinction between human beings and animals or, indeed, artificial intelligence.
4. It challenges the consumerist, materialist culture that dominates in the 21st century, and

5. It is directly relevant to questions of morality and whether there is an absolute distinction between good and evil, right and wrong. These issues have important implications for politics and the media.

The idea that there is something called 'The Eternal', representing not just an eternal extension of time but rather a transcendent order, is an old one, predating the early Greek philosophers. The most ancient of religions affirmed it and gods were worshipped that were seen as controlling transcendent forces. Initially these gods were highly anthropomorphic and were well exemplified in the gods of the Incas, the Norse, the Greeks and the Romans. These gods were powerful but their power was restricted and they were beset by fierce rivalries between each other. They were held to control things that were regarded as mysterious at the time such as the changing cycles of the seasons, fertility and cosmic events such as the movements of the stars and the weather. Sometimes the sun and the moon were worshipped as gods – not surprisingly considering the influence both the moon and the sun had on primitive societies. The return of the sun after the winter solstice brought the promise of longer days, spring, new growth and the warmth that made crops and hunting possible. These were primitive ways of seeking to express the idea of a transcendent realm and the Eternal stood for all those things primitive human beings could not understand. The gods were considered to have power not only over life and death but also over the growing of crops, victory in war and, of course, fertility. Bad harvests or lack of children were blamed on the actions of the gods who were capricious and who had to be placated.

This led to the emergence of a priestly class who exercised great power as they were seen as being in control of the crossing point between human beings and the transcendent world. They built on the myth of these powers by holding secrets and performing rituals which were regarded as the only ways of ensuring that the gods were favourable to the people they represented. Priests and the priestly class therefore became important members of society as they guarded the bridge between the transcendent world and the world of everyday experience. Their power was all the greater as there was no clear demarcation between the transcendent and the material worlds. Gods were to be found everywhere and in all activities of life, and those who neglected the gods or the priests who were their ambassadors did so at their peril. The priests were also the best educated members of society so they were the guardians of the mysteries of writing and had the vision to erect great monuments and temples. They would also claim to prophesy the future and thus give access to secret knowledge which was available nowhere else. Kings and rulers could not ignore them as they represented a transcendent power beyond that of the secular state and they also gave confidence to the population and to soldiers in war as well as to ordinary people in times of prosperity and adversity. For a ruler to ignore the priestly class or the importance of religion was to ignore the main alternative source of authority in the state and thus to make themselves vulnerable to being supplanted. There is a long history of priests determining the fate of kings. An alliance between the rulers and the priests was common for pragmatic reasons. The rulers were interested for their own sake in the powers the priests claimed to represent but were also interested in the powers and authority the priests and religion generally held over their populations. The priests benefitted from the approval and support of the state.

Few within any culture challenged the combined religious and secular order – the combination was simply too powerful and all embracing and, what is more, it made sense of a hard life. Life was unpredictable and cruel. Disease was not understood, death came early in all too many cases and many children died at birth or before they were one year old. Fertility seemed a mystery and only the priests claimed any possible ability to influence child birth. In this seemingly meaningless universe, religion provided a context, a framework and a way of understanding reality. In a very real sense, religion and the priests were 'makers of meaning' and, in their absence, life seemed meaningless, harsh and dark. Religion also provided hope when this was often in short supply. For women who were not married, who could not have children or whose children died, religion provided the possibility that things might be different. The gods could be placated and, perhaps, pleased and might then grant the dearest wish of the supplicant. For men, religion provided the hope of good crops, of protection against adverse conditions and victory in war. Gods like the Roman god Mithras or the Norse God Thor expressed the aspirations of a warrior class and provided the initiate with a sense of belonging to a very exclusive club (initiation into the Mithras cult was by invitation and involved an ordeal which would stretch the bravery of the applicant). Followers of Mithras on both sides of a conflict respected the bravery and kinship of the Mithras followers they were fighting and would endeavour to provide a quick kill to assist the person dying into the afterlife. Belief in an afterlife was strong and, in many cultures, this was assumed to be a continuation of the culture of the present life. Thus followers of Mithras or the war gods of the Norse people both looked forward to banquets, companionship and, of course, a recognition of their bravery. For ordinary people, belief in life after death provided comfort in a world where mortality rates were very high and where most people would die before 35. Belief in a life after death has a very long history with Neolithic grave mounds indicating the state in which Kings and leaders were buried – but even for more humble people the idea of a life after death was an important one. If one believed in life after death, then the death of children or a loved one was not in vain and there could be hope even beyond the grave.

Early religious belief tended to be based on local gods, the gods of the woods and the fields. Ancient 'Hermes', some of the earliest gods with large phalluses, were used as boundary markers and were regarded as blessing the fertility of the fields and family. They were often placed at crossing points where bridges crossed rivers symbolising the crossing between this world and the transcendent or Eternal realm. The ideas of 'family gods' in the East were taken seriously and often this was combined with ancestor worship – the idea that the ancestors of the present generation cared about the currently living family and these ancestors needed to be placated, and could be prayed to and invoked as a way of bringing help in time of need. In many African societies today, the idea that the spirits of the ancestors live on and are closely connected to events among the living is strong. The same is found in traditional Chinese religions such as Confucianism. These concepts were also linked to respect for the old, for their wisdom and understanding and, of course, the old would eventually die and in their turn would become the ancestors to whom supplication could be made and who would be remembered by succeeding generations.

As human understanding developed, so the idea of local gods came to be challenged. The gods were now seen as dwelling in the sky or on top of mountains – they were still anthropomorphic but had powers over nature. The gods quarrelled, had sex and children and had dominion over different parts of the created order: Neptune over the sea, Thor over thunder, Athena over fertility, Mars over war and so on. They also had responsibility for particular aspects of human life – for instance the Greek goddess Hera was responsible for punishing adultery although Zeus, the Father of the Greek gods, readily committed adultery and had sex with both humans and other gods. Some of the gods were capricious such as the Norse God Loki. Knowledge of these gods was preserved by the priests and passed on by story. The stories of the Norse, Greek, Aboriginal, Maori and other gods were preserved in myths that were transmitted by a strong oral tradition and which encapsulated the key insights about how life should be lived. The Greek myths embodied the virtues of a good life, particularly related to bravery, strength, loyalty and fortitude as befitted a people who travelled across the Mediterranean, were in constant conflict and faced ever new challenges. Religion has always been connected with ethical behaviour as the conduct of individuals or communities was seen to directly affect what happened after death as well as succeeding generations. The aboriginal stories are more closely related to 'The Land' and its care and preservation, and these stories explained the origin of the world in which the People lived.

The priestly class in most cultures continued to exercise great influence sometimes 'speaking Truth to power' and standing against kings, queens and the ruling elite, but more often cooperating with them and providing an alternative source of power and influence as well as meaning and hope in an often dark world. However, out of these diverse and vague representations of an Eternal or transcendent order, more sophisticated ideas emerged based largely on the developing idea of a single God.

Religions, therefore, have always stood for an Eternal dimension to reality and to human life but their insights are today largely obscured and marginalised. We live in a world where absolute Truth is derided and relativism dominates. 'Post-Truth' recognises the dominance of the media and the influence of multiple perspectives and narratives. Nevertheless, this book will seek to show that there is a pressing need to express, in the language of today and faced with modern science, sociology and psychology, the enduring relevance of 'The Eternal'. The first step will be to examine the background to the religious imperative which has been such a deep and enduring feature of humanity before seeking to understand why this imperative has become so marginal.

Chapter Two

The Religious Imperative

Traditionally religion and Truth went side by side but the decline in the importance of religion in the Western world has contributed to the decline in the importance of Truth. To understand where we are today, some background is essential as the vast sweep of history has contributed to the rise in prominence of the dragons (cf. p. 1).

The Hebrews were rare in worshipping a single God – initially they were henotheists and worshipped the god of their tribe (thus 'the God of Abraham, Isaac and Jacob') and it was only later that they developed into monotheists. The Hebrew Scriptures are a diverse collection of stories and different genres assembled over time and it seems clear that, initially, there were different names for gods coming from different traditions and the stories from these traditions did not always integrate easily. The God of the Hebrews entered into a binding covenant with what were to become 'the people of Israel' that their God would always, in the long term, protect them provided they worshipped the one God only and were obedient to his commands. In very human fashion, the Hebrew Scriptures record the constant disobedience of the tribes and their leaders, and God's punishment and yet continual faithfulness to the original covenant. The covenant was with the whole people and, therefore, individual failings and sin reflected on the people as a whole and brought the danger of God's punishment. Like other gods of ancient cultures, the god of the Hebrews had to be placated with sacrifices and worship but, above all, absolute obedience and fidelity was demanded. When bad times occurred (whether this be the failure of crops or defeat in battle) this was blamed on lack of fidelity to the Covenant. Any negative effects on the community were not seen as an indictment on their god's failure to protect people but as a just punishment for the people failing to be faithful to the Covenant. The Covenant was with the people of Israel in this life, and the idea of a life after death was undeveloped, vague at best and distinctly unattractive. The promise in the Covenant was not made to individuals but to the people of Israel and their descendants. People lived on through their children and the blessings of God to Abraham (seen as the original father of the Jewish nation) were passed on by lineal descent. Even today, all Jews look to Abraham as their father and being Jewish (except in the rare case of converts) is passed on through the female line as it is always clear who is the mother of a child whereas the identity of the father may be more open to question.

One of the early stories in the Hebrew Scriptures records the destruction of Sodom and Gomorrah by God for their wickedness. Abraham pleaded with God for the life of the citizens even though they were not related to him arguing that it would be unjust to destroy the city if there were, initially, 50, then 40, then 30 and finally just 10 just people in the city. Sodom and Gomorrah were not Israelite cities and this story, perhaps, was the beginning of the understanding that the god of Abraham was not simply another local god but the god of the whole world.

The story of Jonah is largely about the growing realisation that the God of the Hebrews was not just a local God. Jonah was a Hebrew prophet who was told to preach repentance to the city of Nineveh. He refused as he wanted nothing to do with Nineveh. They were not Hebrews, they worshipped other gods and the message of his God, Jonah considered, was not relevant to them. Pursued by his God, he fled to sea only to find the boat in which he travelled overwhelmed by the waves and in danger of sinking. The sailors cast lots to determine who was responsible for the impending catastrophe and the lot fell on Jonah – clearly indicating to them that he was the cause of the storm due to the displeasure of his god. Jonah admitted as much and accepted that his god was punishing him for refusing to obey his commands, so Jonah was thrown overboard. The waves immediately subsided and Jonah, so the story goes, was swallowed by a large fish – eventually being delivered back to dry land. Suitably chastened, Jonah sets out to fulfil God's command and goes to Nineveh. Even then, although he is obedient to the command of his God and preaches the need for repentance his heart does not seem to be in it and he looks forward with anticipation to the destruction of the city of Nineveh for its sin. He sits on a hill outside the city patiently waiting for it to happen. However, not only do the people of the city take his message to heart and repent, but his god forgives them and no destruction takes place. The story marked a key stage in the religious development of the Hebrew people as they came to consider that, whilst they were God's chosen people, their God was nevertheless the God of the whole earth. This was radically countercultural and was an enormous step forward from the worship of local, tribal Gods. The Hebrews still considered that whilst their God was the god of the world, nevertheless they were a specially chosen people in a unique relationship with God which marked them out from all other people.

The people of Israel continually went through great hardship and suffering but their god always remained loyal, and whilst the many civilisations and gods of the ancient world disappeared, the people of Israel survived, worship of their god prospered and their influence increased. It is, indeed, one of the most extraordinary stories in human history that this small group of tribes have largely retained their identity, their beliefs and their traditions over more than three thousand years in a way which almost no other group has done.

Important though the Hebrew insights were, their ideas were initially restricted to their own culture. It was probably the great Persian philosopher Zoroaster who had a greater long-term influence. The date of Zoroaster is not certain and estimates range from earlier than 1500 BCE to 600 BCE. An analysis of the texts seems to make an earlier date more likely. The ideas about the universe of many Greek philosophers may well have emerged from the ideas of Zoroaster which is the Greek name for Zarathustra. Persian tradition says Zoroaster travelled both to India and China so it is quite possible that this key figure influenced both Buddhism and Chinese philosophy. However, the links are not clear as many of Zoroaster's works have been destroyed. There is no doubt that there are links between these different schools of thought and it may be that Zoroaster provides the common ground, but certainty is impossible to achieve. Zoroaster was certainly a very early figure – writing at the very least 600 years before the birth of Jesus and more than a thousand years before the final prophet of Islam, Muhammad.

Zoroaster faced initial opposition but converted a local chieftain to his beliefs, and his beliefs were to form the central part of the religion of three subsequent Persian empires.

Possibly the greatest contribution of Zoroaster, to later thought, was his insistence on a transcendent order and the worship of a single God, Ahura Mazda, who is alone worthy of worship. He was, therefore, a monotheist and he rejected the ideas of his own culture which were based on many gods. He also argued that belief in a single God and living a life of morality and virtue led to a life after death and supreme happiness in the kingdom to come. Although Zoroaster's teaching is monotheistic, he also believed that the supreme God was opposed by an evil power named Ahriman – the followers of Ahriman, having chosen evil instead of justice and goodness, are themselves evil. The precise relationship between the supreme being and the force of evil is unclear, but followers of the two will either come after death to a kingdom of peace and justice or to Ahriman's kingdom which is the Kingdom of the Lie. Those who choose evil are condemned not just by the Great and Wise Lord but by their own conscience and will inhabit the Kingdom of the Lie which is something like the Christian idea of Hell. The strong dualist element of Zoroastrianism, the religion founded by Zoroaster, represents the division between good and evil in both this world and the next. In Zoroaster's own time he saw the peaceful, settled countries as representing good, and the outlaws and robbers representing evil. Once people have made the decision for good and evil there is no going back, no return is possible.

Zoroaster was clear that, apart from the material world around us, there are also spiritual beings who have freedom and these can choose either good or evil; the transcendent or eternal realm was therefore very real. According to Zoroaster individuals have two goals – personal salvation but also the ultimate good for creation as a whole. At the end of time, the good Lord will defeat Ahriman and the present world will come to an end with a wonderful new world full of peace and justice.

These ideas, some scholars claim, may have had a strong influence in the West. In early Judaism there was no idea of life after death. Their god made promises to Abraham and his descendants. Some scholars suggest that personal immortality first came into Jewish thought at the time of the Maccabean rebellion (c 167–160 BCE) when many Jews were slaughtered by the occupying forces. In its early years of development, Hebrew ideas saw people living on in their children and, whilst there was an afterlife in 'Sheol', it was an unsatisfactory existence and was a pale reflection of this life. It was certainly not a state to which anyone aspired. After the rebellion of the Maccabees against the Seleucid empire and with the death of many thousands of young Jewish men, Jewish thinkers felt the need for some life after death but may also have been influenced by Zoroastrian thought. Some writers also consider that Christian ideas of the Fall and of Heaven and Hell as well as a final judgement may be strongly influenced by Zoroastrian beliefs.

Zoroaster may have been the first to proclaim belief in

one God (others will argue that Abraham was the first – but this depends on the uncertain dating of both Zoroaster and Abraham). He proclaimed a message for all people and held that every human being was equal irrespective of race, gender or nationality. Zoroaster's writings are held to have been inspired by God, but unlike the Prophet Muhammad in Islam, he was not a passive recipient of God's message. According to Zoroaster each individual has to struggle towards God and be active in trying to understand God. Zoroaster was never, ever, considered a god – he was fully human.

In spite of the enormous influence that Zoroaster may have had on Western and Eastern thought, the number of Zoroastrians today are few, mainly confined to a group called Parsees in India and in the Indian diaspora. There are only perhaps 140,000 Parsees remaining. This is because they refuse to accept converts, and with a falling birth rate numbers are also falling. However, Zoroaster's emphasis on a single God and on a transcendent order represented a real move away from the local gods of particular cultures, although these continued for more than a thousand years to be the dominant religious idea. Nevertheless, in whatever form, the idea of a transcendent order that could affect the material world was widely accepted however this reality may have been expressed.

The gods of ancient Egypt were diverse and changed with different dynasties, but the idea of an eternal realm was generally accepted. The idea of a single God was a very early development – the One, self-begotten, and self-existent god can be traced to at least 3500 BCE. Initially, the supreme God was Ra, the sun God, but in time, Osiris, the king of the underworld and judge of the dead, became the equal and, in certain cases, the superior of Ra. Osiris, supported by a range of other deities, increasingly took on the paramount role for ensuring 'everlasting life and resurrection' through his judgement of the dead. Eternal life centred on the soul and spirit, leaving the body behind.

Egyptians believed that a human being was made up of both physical and spiritual aspects. As well as the body, each person had a šwt (shadow), a ba (soul) and a ka (life force). The heart was thought to be the seat of thoughts and emotions and after death the spiritual aspects of the person were released and could move freely, but they were incomplete and needed the physical remains of the body (or possibly a statue) as a permanent home. The ultimate goal of the deceased was to reunite the ka and ba living on as an 'akh', or 'effective one'.

The practice of mummification, of preserving the body at death and of adding food and other materials for an afterlife, is explained by the afterlife taking a bodily form. The new body effectively grows like a seed from the old body (hence the importance of mummification and the preservation of the corpse of wealthy individuals).

Beliefs in the gods and in the afterlife were central to ancient Egyptian civilisation from its inception and the rule of the Pharaohs was based on the divine right of kings. The Egyptian gods had supernatural powers and were called on for help or protection. However, the gods were not always viewed as benevolent, and sacrifices and prayers were needed to appease them. Failure of crops, lack of fertility or problems with the flooding of the Nile delta (on which the Egyptians depended) were all seen as punishments by the gods. The structure of the Egyptian pantheon of gods changed continually as new deities were promoted but priests made little effort to bring together and to synchronize the diverse and sometimes conflicting myths. These various conceptions of gods were not considered contradictory but rather layers in the multiple facets of a transcendent or Eternal reality.

Gods were worshipped largely by priests in temples which contained a shrine containing a statue or statues of the god or gods. Temples were generally not places of public worship but private places kept by the priests who made offerings on behalf of the people. The Pharaoh was often seen as the intermediary between the gods and the people of Egypt although this varied over time. Nevertheless, the blessing and support of the gods was essential for any Pharaoh to prosper and be secure.

Egyptian ideas of a single God and survival of death may well have influenced Hebrew and later Christian thought about life after death, and may also have affected Plato. Influences from Zoroastrianism and Egyptian ideas, therefore, may both have been factors although it is impossible at this distance in time to have any clarity about where the lines of influence lay. At the least it is clear that ideas of life after death were common in ancient cultures.

Greek philosophy was generally sceptical about the anthropomorphic gods of its culture. The major philosophers, deriving particularly from Pythagoras, were interested in the nature of reality and often saw mathematics as giving the best insight into the real world which was distinguished from the world of appearance. Socrates, who was Plato's teacher, was put on trial by the free citizens of Athens on two charges – atheism and corrupting the young. The charge of atheism rested on Socrates' dismissal of the anthropomorphic Greek Gods with their petty jealousies and rivals. These were, he considered, myths which might satisfy common people but they could not stand up to rational examination. The charge of corrupting the young rested on Socrates' passion for helping young people to think for themselves and to challenge the wisdom of their parents – something which the middle-class parents of Athens did not welcome (as happens also in today's society).

Socrates, and his pupil Plato, most certainly believed in a transcendent order – they were the very opposite of materialists. They were committed to belief in life after death and they were dualists, believing in the survival of the soul. Plato said that the highest duty of a human being was to be a 'lover' of the soul – to care for his or her soul which was immortal and which would survive death. In all the actions a human being performed, the soul is either being damaged or developed and, therefore, the rational person will not be concerned with outwards 'goods' such as money or possessions but will instead be concerned with developing and preserving their soul. Socrates was condemned to death on the two charges set against him and was made to swallow the poison hemlock. He could have easily escaped but, having lived all his life under the laws of Athens, he was quite content to die under these same laws. He was given time to prepare for death and he swallowed the poison whilst his friends grieved. Socrates, by contrast, had no fear of death – he staked his whole life in his belief in the immortality of the soul and faced his death peacefully.

Socrates and Plato represent possibly the clearest idea of a transcendent reality divorced from any idea of gods. They argued for an Eternal order which is the most ultimately real and true part of the universe, and of which the material world around us is a mere shadow. This material world is a pale reflection of ultimate reality. Plato argued that everything we see around us is like a shadow which is impermanent, changing and a pale reflection of true reality. Plato sets his position out clearly in his story of the Cave (*Republic* 514a–520a).

He asks us to imagine people living in an underground cave with their backs to the mouth of the cave – they are tied to chairs and cannot move or turn round and can only see the back wall of the cave. Behind them, between the entrance to the cave and where they are sitting, is a high wall and behind that wall pass human-like creatures, holding up various figures above the top of the wall. There is a roaring fire behind these figures and this casts flickering shadows on to the back wall of the cave. The only thing these cave dwellers see is shadow play – the shadows of images of reality. They have sat in this position since they were born and think that what they see is real.

Plato's story suggests that one cave dweller uses reason to

release himself from the bonds that tie him to his chair and to stand up and ask where all the shadows come from. He turns around and sees the figures being held up above the wall. Initially he is perplexed but he walks backwards towards the entrance to the cave and sees the wall, the moving figures and the fire – eventually he comes to the entrance to the cave and he goes outside. Initially he is dazzled by the sharp sunlight and the power of the sun. For Plato, the sun is the 'Form' of the good – true reality itself in comparison with which everything in the cave is a dim shadow. The Forms (of the Good, the Just, the True) represent the absolute reality which exists timelessly and spacelessly, and it is these that the pale shadows on earth dimly represent. So when humans talk of justice, beauty or goodness they are referring to the pale reality of these ideas in this world which dimly represent the absolute ideas of the Just, the Beautiful and the Good. These absolute ideas are transcendent and Eternal.

The cave dweller who has managed to leave the cave decides he has a duty to tell the others and he re-enters the cave to tell them of the prison in which they are living and that the shadows on the cave wall which they take to be the real world are, in fact, only the flickering reflections of 'real' things. Their reaction, however, is to become angry – they refuse to accept his interpretation and see him as challenging their way of looking at the world in which they have lived for so long and which they find so comfortable. As he insists on his view, their anger increases. They not only do not believe him, but in the end they turn on him and kill him. Plato maintains that this will be the destiny of the philosopher who attempts to challenge the comfortable view of 'reality' held by the majority of people. He had, of course, seen his teacher and his friend, Socrates, put to death in exactly this way by the Athenian crowd so he had good reason for his views.

The task of the philosopher is to be free from the cave-like world of sense experience which is the material reality in which one is trapped and to look beyond the darkness of the cave, which our present world represents, to the true reality which can be seen outside it. This was the basis for the film *The Matrix*, which portrays human beings as living in a world of illusion and the task of coming to understand true reality as a painful and hard one. Similar themes emerge in Buddhism. Tenzin Palmo was a British female Buddhist monk, and in her book *Cave in the Snow* she recounts a dream she had whilst living in a cave in the high Himalayas. Arguably it revealed more than anything she said about the level of spiritual development she had reached.

I was in a prison, a vast prison composed of many different levels. On the top floor people were living in luxury, in penthouse type splendour, while in the basement others were undergoing terrible torture. In the intermediate floors the rest of the inhabitants were engaged in various activities in diverse conditions. Suddenly I realised that no matter what level people were on we were all nevertheless trapped in a prison. With that I found a boat and decided to escape taking as many people as I could with me. I went all over the prison telling people of their predicament and urging them to break free. But no matter how hard I tried, they all seemed to be locked in an awful inertia and in the end only two people had the courage and the will to come with me. We got into the boat, and even though there were prison guards around, nobody stopped us as we sailed out of the prison to the world outside. Once we were there we started to run alongside the prison. As I looked over at it I could still see all the people in the windows busily engaged in their different activities, not the least bit concerned about the truth of their activities. We ran for miles and miles on a path parallel to the prison which seemed never ending. I became increasingly exhausted and dispirited. I felt I was never going to get beyond the prison and that we might as well return and go back in. I was about to give up when I realised the two other people who had followed me out had their hopes pinned on me and that if I gave up they would be doomed as well. I couldn't let them down so I kept going. Immediately we came to a T-junction beyond which was a completely different landscape. It was like suburbia. There were these neat houses with flowery borders and trees. We came to the first house and knocked at the door. A nice middle-aged woman opened it, looked at us, "Oh, you've come from that place. Not many people get out. You'll be OK now but you must change your clothes. To go back would be dangerous, but you must try to help others also to get out." At that point I had a great surge of aspiration. "I have tried but no-one wants to come," I told the woman. She replied, "Those in power will be helping you." At that I said, "I dedicate myself to working with them so that I can help free all beings." I woke up at that point and giggled at the image of the middle-aged lady in suburbia.

The dream was clear. In her subconscious, Tenzin Palmo had pledged herself to lead the great escape out of the prison of samsara, the realms of suffering existence we are condemned to until we reach the eternal freedom of Enlightenment. She had also internalised, it seemed, the Bodhisattva ideal of unconditioned altruism. This is similar to Plato's story of the cave. Both see an Eternal realm as being of profound and ultimate significance but neither identify it with God or the gods.

For Plato, ultimate reality lies in the ideal world of the Forms – these are the ultimate absolutes which exist beyond time and space. When we see in the world examples of goodness, justice or beauty, we call things by these names because they participate in or in some way resemble the absolute ideas of the Good, the Just and the Beautiful which exist beyond time and space. The transcendent world of the Forms represents ultimate reality in comparison with which the material world of change is a shadow. Plato, therefore, sets out a transcendent world in comparison with which the material world we experience every day is a pale illusion.

On death, Plato argues that human souls leave their body and then have to account before 'the judges' for the life they have lived and they then decide into which body they will next be born. Plato, therefore, believed in reincarnation into another human body. This was the basis for his idea that knowledge was actually recollection of things that we once knew but have forgotten.

An extract from Wordsworth's poem *Ode on Intimations to Immortality* puts it well:

Our birth is but a sleep and a forgetting:
The Soul that rises with us, our life's Star,
Hath had elsewhere its setting,
And cometh from afar:
Not in entire forgetfulness,
And not in utter nakedness,
But trailing clouds of glory do we come
From God, who is our home:
Heaven lies about us in our infancy!

Shades of the prison-house begin to close
Upon the growing Boy,
But he beholds the light, and whence it flows,
He sees it in his joy;
The Youth, who daily farther from the east
Must travel, still is Nature's Priest,
And by the vision splendid
Is on his way attended;
At length the Man perceives it die away,
And fade into the light of common day.

For Plato we can, in childhood, remember something of our previous lives but these memories quickly fade and we are surrounded by the mundane and everyday world which we take to be the only reality. Plato's god the Demiurge was a craftsman who brought order out of chaos. He did not create matter but fashioned it using the absolute idea of the Forms as his model. Nevertheless, the chaotic matter resisted his will and this is the reason for the lack of perfection in the world. The Demiurge is not a god to be worshipped – rather the Eternal was to be found in living the ethical life and striving for 'the Good'.

Although Plato's influence was profound his brightest pupil, Aristotle, did not accept his world-view. Aristotle started the West on the scientific path. He worked from observation and had no idea of a life after death (except in one disputed text which most scholars did not think was written by Aristotle). Aristotle has no need for the idea of God except as a 'prime mover' needed only to explain motion in the universe. God, for Aristotle, is timeless, spaceless, utterly immutable, bodiless and does not create or sustain the universe. God has, for Aristotle, no interest in the Universe and yet is supremely happy because God contemplates god's self. However, merely by existing, this god draws the universe towards himself and thereby causes motion.

Plato and Aristotle have dominated philosophy ever since and both have been hugely influential but it is Aristotle's empirical approach that was to have the longer lasting and greater influence. Both Plato and Aristotle were to have a profound influence on Christianity and Islam.

Two thousand years ago, at the time of Jesus of Nazareth, few doubted the existence of a transcendent order whether this was seen as represented by the God of the Hebrews, the Gods of Rome or Greece or the transcendent order of Socrates and Plato. The world was considered to be governed by forces that human beings could only dimly comprehend but the reality of a transcendent or eternal dimension to reality was unquestioned.

Jesus of Nazareth certainly affirmed this transcendent order. He was a devout Jew and the existence of God as well as the existence of angels and devils seemed unquestioned. The Christian tradition holds that Jesus had the power to perform miracles that violated the material order and the central Christian claim is that he survived death on the cross and, in so doing, opened the door for his followers to also survive death and to live with him in a heavenly realm. Jesus ushered in nearly two thousand years of continuing and developing Christian history and, throughout this time until comparatively recently, the existence of a transcendent order was relatively unquestioned.

St Paul, one of the most important interpreters and possibly formulators of Christian ideas, affirmed the existence of a transcendent realm, as well as did the great Church Fathers such as Irenaeus, Tertullian, Origin, Augustine and many, many others all affirm the existence of a transcendent realm. Even those who put forward alternative positions in the first three centuries when Christianity was being formed, such as the Gnostics, the Manicheans, the Donatists and the Arians, all agreed that there was a life after death and a transcendental dimension to life.

Christians have always been beset by splits and schisms of which the most important was the great divide between the Western and Eastern Orthodox churches in 1054, and the Protestant Reformation which gave rise to myriad different Church groups. All, however, were united in affirming a life after death although understandings of this varied widely. Much depended on different understandings of the nature of God. As a generalisation, the Catholic tradition followed Aristotle (as mediated through St Thomas Aquinas) and saw God as immutable, timeless, spaceless and bodiless. This led to the final end for the Catholic being seen as the Beatific Vision of God. In most Protestant theology, God is seen as personal and temporal, and this leads to the idea of a temporal heaven after death. Both traditions also have the idea of permanent exile from God.

In Islam belief in an afterlife is also strong. When the prophet Muhammad was born, all the tribes of Arabia had their own gods, and loyalty to these gods was fierce and often gave rise to conflict. The city of Mekka was the only place where all the tribes could gather together and trade peacefully as they all had representations of their gods in the Kabbah (the ancient shrine at the centre of Mekka) and there was an agreement that no fighting was allowed in Mekka which, of course, was very useful in adding to the trade and prosperity of the city. Even when the prophet proclaimed his message of a single God and the claimed divine revelation of the text of the Qur'an his message, whilst challenging to the myriad supporters of the tribal gods since it emphasised the unity of God and the oneness of God, was nevertheless understandable as it still affirmed a transcendent dimension to life. Islam affirms the existence of countless millions of angels and, above all, a life after death in a heavenly paradise as well as the possibility of permanent exile from God dependent on the conduct of individuals in this life. Angels keep a permanent record of the good and bad actions of each individual and will report on them at the end of each person's life.

Throughout recorded history, therefore, the existence of a transcendent dimension to reality has been near universally affirmed and a life after death proclaimed and has been part of a claim to a truthful understanding of reality. Today, at least in the West (particularly in Europe, Australasia and parts of North America), the whole idea is rejected or greeted with incredulity. How has this come about?

Chapter Three

The Rise of Atheism

The claim to the existence of absolute truth has traditionally been associated with the idea of gods or a God which provided an underpinning for all truth claims. There is nevertheless a long tradition of rejecting such a religious perspective. Atheism has a long history – Socrates was accused of being an atheist because he rejected the state gods of Athens, the prophet Muhammad was accused of being an atheist because he rejected tribal gods. Atheism has long been a pejorative term applied to anyone who rejects the currently accepted religious views. However, atheism as a term used to reject all gods and any idea of an Eternal or transcendent realm has also existed since the beginning of recorded time – albeit as a minority position. The influential Islamic philosopher Al-Ghazali attacked the materialists of his time who were effectively forerunners of modern-day atheists, and Greek and Roman philosophies both had their share of atheists.

The great poet Al-Ma'arri denounced superstition and dogmatism in religion, arguing that Islam had no greater claim to truth than any other religious tradition. A sceptic and a pessimist, he held surprisingly modern views, being a committed vegetarian and arguing in favour of birth control. Like Al-Rawandi and Al-Razi, Al-Ma'arri dismissed the plausibility of prophecy and observed that religions are all used by the powerful to control the weak. He wrote:

> … do not suppose the statements of the prophets to be true; they are all fabrications. Men lived comfortably till they came and spoiled life. The sacred books are only such a set of idle tales as any age could have and indeed did actually produce…

They all err – Moslems, Christians, Jews, and Magians (Zoroastrians): Two make Humanity's universal sect: One man intelligent without religion, And, one religious without intellect.

(*The Epistle of Forgiveness* [*Resalat Al-Ghufran* رسالة الغفران])

Al-Ma'arri's point was that religions are generally destructive, and the cause of great social conflict and personal unhappiness has been taken up by many since – for instance Thomas Jefferson, who noted:

Millions of innocent men, women, and children, since the introduction of Christianity, have been burned, tortured, fined, and imprisoned, yet we have not advanced one inch toward uniformity. What has been the effect of coercion? To make one half of the world fools and the other half hypocrites...

(*Notes on the State of Virginia*, 1780)

As Al-Ma'arri wrote:

You said, "A wise one created us"; That may be true, we would agree. "Outside of time and space," you postulate. Then why not say at once that you propound a mystery immense, Which tells us of our lack of sense?

From the 17th century onwards, science began to rise as an independent discipline – although the discoveries of Copernicus and Galileo had previously challenged the old, religious understanding of the Universe for instance that the earth was fixed motionless in space and that the 'heavens' revolved around the earth, or that the stars were set in spheres that revolved around the earth.

At first scientific discoveries were made by people who

believed in God and saw themselves uncovering the glory of God's creation – they were 'natural philosophers' who saw no distinction between science (which did not emerge as a term until the 1830s), philosophy and theology. Many of the greatest early scientists were religious – for instance the Catholic religious order the Society of Jesus (the Jesuits) had some of the top astronomers and mathematicians in the Western world. Surprisingly 36 craters on the moon are named for their Jesuit discoverers. Soon, however, science began to emerge as an independent discipline and began to explain things that had previously been the province of religion. Whereas once the world was seen as mysterious with God's hand and miracles everywhere, increasingly science explained how things worked (e.g. illness and pregnancy; thunder and cyclones) and religious explanations became increasingly marginal.

Because scientific knowledge was limited, the effects were at first confined largely to an educated elite and the control of the Church was very strong. There is a long tradition of European humanism stemming from Erasmus and Thomas More. Utilitarians such as Bentham, JS Mill as well as TS Eliot and European thinkers tried to develop a rational 'religion of humanity' which embraced Christian moral principles without the foundation of belief in God or the difficult, maybe embarrassing texts and traditions of the past. AA Milne wrote:

> The Old Testament is responsible for more atheism, agnosticism and disbelief – call it what you will – than any book ever written; it has emptied more churches than all the counter-attractions of cinema, motor bicycle and the golf course. (cited in *2000 Years of Disbelief* by James A. Haught)

Under humanism, people could be philosophical atheists but not lead 'Godless' lives. All this was a prelude to modern atheism.

The term 'atheism' is imprecise. Speculative atheism is the

philosophic position which maintains that it is possible to prove the non-existence of God. This tends to be confined to a relatively small number of academic philosophers since proving a negative is always difficult. Protest atheism, stemming from Dostoyevsky's character of Ivan Karamazov in *The Brothers Karamazov*, accepts the existence of God but rejects God on the grounds of the unmerited suffering of innocent human beings. Far more prevalent and, indeed, the norm in Western society is practical atheism where people's lives effectively deny the existence of gods or any transcendent realm.

In the past three hundred years, however, things have changed and there has been a rising tide of practical atheism, reinforced by speculative atheism, which has carried nearly everything before it. There has been no single starting point although philosophers such as David Hume (1711–1776) had a profound and lasting effect – particularly, in the case of Hume, with his attack on attempts to prove the existence of God. Hume was also a forerunner of verificationism: He wished to burn all books on theology since, as they contained no experimental reasoning and no mathematical reasoning, their claims were meaningless. He wrote:

> When we run over libraries... if we take in our hand any volume of divinity... let us ask, "Does it contain any abstract reasoning concerning quantity or number?" No. "Does it contain any experimental reasoning concerning matter of fact and existence?" No. Commit it to the flames then for it can contain nothing not sophistry and illusion.
> (*An Enquiry concerning Human Understanding*)

Hume was to profoundly influence Immanuel Kant who, whilst being a Lutheran, has had an even greater impact. Immanuel Kant (1724–1804) said that Hume "awoke him from his dogmatic slumbers" and he agreed with Hume that knowledge could only come through the senses but, unlike Hume, he left room for God and a transcendent dimension to reality. Kant sought to develop a complete critical philosophy which depended on the primacy of reason. He postulated the existence of God to explain the existence of freedom, reason and order in the universe (all of which he acknowledged were assumptions), but he dismissed any possibility of proving God's existence. Kant's God was, essentially, fairly remote – needed to guarantee order in the universe but little else. Later in life, Kant produced a series of four essays under the title *Religion Within the Boundaries of Reason Alone* (1794). These presented the case for believing in God as the most sensible postulate to explain the way things are, but they also revealed the doubts that plagued Kant.

He argued that human beings can only know the world of phenomena – the world as it is seen through the spectacles of space and time which constitute the human frame of reference through which all reality is seen (and which therefore agreed with Hume's empirical analysis). The world is intelligible only by causal relations between events in the world. Knowledge of God is not possible but, for Kant, God's existence is a necessary postulate if key assumptions are made including the fairness and rationality of the universe. Kant had devoted little space to discussion of either any transcendent realm or of religious experience – which is not the same as saying that Kant ruled out the transcendent. Rather, Kant claimed that any transcendent realm is in principle unknowable: The noumenal world, reality as it really is independent of human senses, is in principle inaccessible. The only reality reachable by human beings is that known through our five senses. Kant rejected the possibility of religious experience since God is not an object in space and time and can, therefore, not be experienced by the five senses of human beings.

Whilst Kant believed in God, he did not think that the God in which he believed had any effect on the world – except in one important sense. Morality, he held, was based on reason alone and God wanted humans to act according to reason. Any idea, therefore, of a transcendent perspective on reality, even if it existed, was irrelevant to human life for Kant. However, there was one major exception to this which most Kantian scholars gloss over as if Kant had made an unfortunate error in introducing it.

Kant argued that human beings are animals but with a capacity to reason and with free will. When human beings act according to their animal nature, they deny what is supreme in humanity namely the capacity to reason. The fully human person, the person who fulfils their true potential as a human being, is one who always acts according to reason and not according to instinct. Kant, as a Lutheran, argued that when human beings act according to their animal nature (which everyone does at some stage in their life) they put themselves in bondage to a lack of rationality – they effectively create a prison of their own making from which they are unable to free themselves. They thus fall into the grip of what Kant calls "Radical Evil". Kant argues that since all human beings have fallen into the trap they are imprisoned by the choice they have made to deny reason. They have placed themselves in bondage to their animal nature. They are, therefore, unable to free themselves and God is needed to release them through God becoming human in the Christian idea of the incarnation. Kant is putting forward what comes close to the Christian idea of original sin which St Augustine and others argued was inherited from the sin of disobedience by Adam and Eve in the garden of Eden. For Kant, the prison of radical evil is a prison of our own making yet, in both cases, God needed to become incarnate as a free gift of love to release human beings from the effects of their animal and therefore selfish behaviour.

The significance of Kant was to make God irrelevant to ethics except in the one area just outlined – Goethe was to attack Kant for "besmirching his philosopher's cloak with the filthy stain of radical evil after he had taken many a long year to rid himself of this dirty prejudice". Goethe's language was extreme as he recognised that Kant had compromised his wholly rational approach by bringing in the idea of Radical Evil and most subsequent philosophers have tended to ignore this aspect of his thought (Michalson in *Fallen Freedom* [Cambridge University Press, 2008] is an honourable exception).

Gordon Michalson argues that there was a "divide in the road" after Kant.

1. Some rejecting God and seeking to account for the universe and how to act within it through reason alone. This became the dominant position in Western culture.
2. Others accepting that faith goes beyond reason and relying on revelation to support belief in God.

Auguste Comte (1798–1857) built on the idea of secular rationalism which Kant had pioneered. Compte is regarded as the 'founding father' of the science of society or sociology, and he was the first to use the term 'sociology'. Comte rejected the individualism of Kant but he accepted Kant's view that knowledge can only be obtained through the senses. Compte, like Kant, rejected metaphysics or any attempt to postulate a realm beyond the physical. Compte argued that civilisations have a three stage intellectual and social evolution moving from a theological approach which involved gods to metaphysics and finally to a positive approach based on the science of human behaviour.

Science forces forward this evolution, until eventually humans turn to knowledge of humankind itself leaving behind any primitive ideas of a transcendent realm. Compte believed that the scientific method of sociology would be the ultimate expression of the final scientific stage in which reliable empirical and reasoned knowledge would be evident providing scientific data about human behaviours. Compte argued that this latter stage would replace the need for religion, particularly as this stage would move away from knowledge informed by theology and metaphysics. Later Compte recognised the cohesive function that religion played in society, and he argued for a new secular religion. This new religion of humanity would perform the same function as the old religions, but it would be based on scientific and rational sociology. This new rationality is, he claimed, the foundation on which sociology is built and it heavily influenced the work of Durkheim, Marx and Weber. All three considered religion to be central to the study and understanding of humankind. They placed religion at the very core of sociology, as it was an important way of comprehending the universe for many people, and so deserved their study.

Sociologists claim that it is the answers people arrive at which often tell us more about those seeking the answers than they do about dispassionate enquiry. The motive for asking certain questions often leads to the answers desired by those who ask the question – there is frequently an implicit agenda in place. As an example, in the history of science different ways of looking at the world are promoted at certain times and these serve particular agendas:

- The idea of the earth being at the centre of the Universe and all stars moving round it fitted perfectly with a religious model which saw the world as one in which God created the first man and woman at the centre of the universe.

- A picture which allowed human beings to exploit nature through mechanisation fitted with the mechanistic universe which arose around the time of Newton.

- Humans being treated as means rather than as ends in themselves leads to a focus on a scientific understanding of human nature.

- Concentration on people being dehumanised in the workplace (for instance through talk of 'human resources' to describe those who employ, control, manage and dismiss people) fits in well with genetics and explaining in almost mechanistic terms what it is to be human. This contributes to the real risk of 'dehumanising' people – thus leading to individuals being regarded as of little intrinsic worth. They become means to an end of greater profit or production for the few – their humanity is denied and this has inevitable consequences.

Ludwig Feuerbach (1804–1872) argued that human beings are essentially animals. In *The Essence of Christianity* he argues that God is a projection of human need and the fear of being alone in a universe devoid of meaning. Feuerbach was essentially an anthropologist and a materialist – he said that "man is what he eats". Human beings are made up of matter and nothing else. Feuerbach argues that the idea of God is a projection of human nature. God is seen as essentially an idealised version of what a human being could be at its best. Human beings are not capable of achieving perfection so they project on to the idea of God all those qualities which they would like to have but do not. God is seen to be perfect and free from sin whilst humans are imperfect and mired in sin; God is omnipotent whilst human power is limited; God is omniscient whilst human knowledge is limited.

Feuerbach sets a high value to morality but does not consider it to be grounded in God, rather God is the projection of an idealised morality. The idea of God has to be supremely good and perfect as otherwise the idea of God would not embody the total of human aspirations: "We have reduced the otherworldly, supernatural and superhuman essence of god to its particular foundations in the essence of man. Thus we have in the end arrived back at our starting point. Man is the beginning of religion, Man is the centre of religion, Man is the end of religion." So instead of humans being made in the image of God, human beings make God in their own idealised image.

Feuerbach says that, "Religion is the dream of the human mind." (Preface to the Second Edition of *The Essence of Christianity*) Feuerbach's views were not popular at the time when to be an atheist was considered socially unacceptable but he said: "I would rather be a devil in alliance with truth, than an angel in alliance with falsehood." Feuerbach was to profoundly influence others including Darwin, Nietzsche and Freud.

Sigmund Freud's (1856–1939) emphasis lay on the sexual development of human beings: Human beings, he claimed, can get stuck in one or other of their early stages of early sexual development. Freud analysed the paintings and writings of Christopher Haizmann, a seventeenth century painter who considered that he had a pact with the devil. It is of interest that whilst Christopher Haizmann believed he had such a pact, Freud calls it a neurosis, which means that he believed that the so-called 'pact' could be explained by psychological factors. Freud did not look outside of the human mind for the devil or any force of evil. Evil instead was something that Freud explained entirely in terms of the subconscious mind.

Freud argued that God was a projected father figure (Feuerbach's influence is clear here). The child experienced the real father as the source of fear and guilt, yet the child wants unconditional love from the same figure. All human beings long for an unconditional, loving father figure who can accept them as they are and forgive all the dark sides of their character, so the religious idea of God is a projection of the human imagination and is the means whereby humans cope with the lack of love and the lack of meaning in the world. "At bottom God is nothing more than an exalted father." (*Totem and Taboo: Resemblances Between the Mental Lives of Savages and Neurotics*, 1913)

Freud argues that human psychological development is related to how we navigate various sexual stages. In his *Three Essays on the Theory of Sexuality* (1915), Freud outlined five stages of manifestations of the sexual drive: Oral, Anal, Phallic, Latency, and Genital. At each stage, different areas of the child's body become the focus of pleasure and the dominant source of sexual arousal. Differences in satisfying the sexual urges at each stage will inevitably lead to differences in adult personalities. Conflicts between the sex drive and rules of society are present at every stage.

Freud saw Judaism as a perfect example of his theory that God was a Father figure projection.

"The Mosaic religion had been a Father religion; Christianity became a Son religion. The old God, the Father, took second place; Christ, the Son, stood in His stead, just as in those dark times every son had longed to do." (*Moses and Monotheism*, 1938) Psychology requires individuals to come to recognise the psychological forces that gave rise to religion and, in so doing, to free themselves.

Religion is an attempt to get control over the sensory world, in which we are placed, by means of the wish-world which we have developed inside us as a result of biological and psychological necessities. [...] If one attempts to assign to religion its place in man's evolution, it seems not so much to be a lasting acquisition, as a parallel to the neurosis which the civilized individual must pass through on his way from childhood to maturity.

(Freud, *Moses and Monotheism*, 1939)

Émile Durkheim (1858–1917) was influenced by Compte but also by previous French secular thinking in the 18th century. French secular thinkers had grappled with how morality could be maintained without religion. They had asked, just like Dostoyevsky's Ivan Karamazov: "Once God is dead, is everything permissible?" Durkheim thought much of Compte's work too speculative and vague. To become scientific, according to Durkheim, sociology must study "social facts" – it must pursue the analysis of social institutions with the same objectivity as scientists study nature. Durkheim's famous first principle of sociology is: "Study social facts as things!" By this he means that social life can be analysed as rigorously as objects or events in nature. Durkheim was concerned with a similar problem. In the past, he argued, religion had held society together – leading people to a common devotion to sacred things rather than mundane, day to day existence. Now that, in a rational age, religion was dying, what was to take its place?

Durkheim analyses institutions in terms of their functions. Thus: "The determination of function is… necessary for the complete explanation of the phenomena… To explain a social fact it is not enough to show the cause on which it depends; we must also, at least in most cases, show its function in the establishment of social order." Durkheim sought two things:

1) An understanding of the origin and causes of social institutions, and
2) An understanding of their function.

Durkheim sees religion as a communal phenomenon rather than individual. Religion is:

a system of ideas by which the individual represents to themselves the society of which they are all members, and the obscure but intimate relations which they have with it. (Durkheim, 1915, cited in Hamilton, 1995, p. 101)

A religion is a unified system of beliefs and practices relative to sacred things, that is to say, things set apart and forbidden

– beliefs and practices which unite in one single moral community called a Church, all those who adhere to them.

Unlike William James (1842–1910), Durkheim was not concerned with the variety of religious experience of individuals but rather with the communal activity and the communal bonds generated by taking part in religious activities. Harry Alpert classified Durkheim's four major functions of religion as providing the following social forces:

1. Disciplinary – religious rituals impose self-discipline and control.
2. Cohesive – religious ceremonies bring people together to affirm their common bonds.
3. Vitalizing – religious observance gives new life to the social heritage of the group.
4. Euphoric – religion helps to counteract depression and giving a sense of well-being and the rightness of their moral world.

Religion can also bring about social change – norms can be critically examined and challenged by reference to "God's law". It also marks the individual's passage through life – e.g. the rituals of baptism, marriage and death.

Probably more influential than sociological or psychological theorists was the influence of atheist philosophers who dismissed talk of God as meaningless. Perhaps the most important were Moritz Schlick (1882–1936), the Vienna Circle and AJ Ayer who gave rise to logical positivism. Ayer was a verificationist and insisted that the only way to make meaningful statements was to ensure that any statement could, in principle, be verified using sense experience. He said:

The criterion which we use to test the genuineness of apparent statements of fact is the criterion of verifiability. We say that a sentence is factually significant to any given person if, and only if, he knows how to verify the proposition which it purports to describe – that is, if he knows what observations would lead him, under certain conditions, to accept the proposition as being true or reject it as being false.

(AJ Ayer, *Language, Truth and Logic*, p. 35)

This was significant and became, and still is, very influential. The claim being made is that for any statement to have any meaning requires evidence and the only evidence that would be acceptable is evidence that can be replicated in the laboratory or in similar testable conditions. The consequences of this are profound. Any statement about ethics, aesthetics, God or any transcendent realm is rendered meaningless (note not false – since the statement is meaningless it makes no sense to speak of truth or falsity).

The other side of verificationism is falsificationism which was argued for by Antony Flew (1923–1910). Any statement is meaningless unless it can be falsified. If a claim is made and no evidence will be accepted against it, then the claim is devoid of content, it is meaningless. If, for instance, someone claims that another person loves them and would not accept any evidence to counter the claim, the claim has no meaning. Similarly, Flew holds, religious statements are meaningless. He asks: "What would have to occur or to have occurred to constitute for you a disproof of the love of, or of the existence of, God?" If the believer will not accept any evidence to counter the claim, then the claim is devoid of meaning. Falsificationism is important as science advances by previous theories being shown to be false, and if nothing will count against a claim, then it is persuasive to argue that the claim has no meaning.

Verificationism and Falsificationism lie beneath current atheist approaches. They reject claims to a transcendental dimension or to the Eternal as simply devoid of meaning. No evidence (meaning evidence that can be replicated) can be produced in favour of or against the claims so the claims are devoid of meaning. Behind almost all of modern atheism lies verificationism and falsificationism.

Taken together, the forces of psychology, sociology and philosophy have marginalised religion by reducing it to a product of human striving. They have emptied the call of the Eternal of any content by rendering discussion of it as meaningless. We are left with the world of the everyday, the material world in which we live and move and have our being. Nothing beside remains. The result has been the decline of religion and this was well expressed in the poem "Dover Beach" (1867) by Matthew Arnold as the following extract makes clear:

> The Sea of Faith
> Was once, too, at the full, and round earth's shore
> Lay like the folds of a bright girdle furled.
> But now I only hear
> Its melancholy, long, withdrawing roar,
> Retreating, to the breath
> Of the night-wind, down the vast edges drear
> And naked shingles of the world.

This is a fair reflection of the modern world's lack of interest in any transcendent or Eternal dimension in life. Psychology, sociology and anthropology regard religion as something primitive – something to be studied as affecting community cohesion and perhaps psychological well-being but nothing more. In all this, the original basis for religion and, indeed, for the priests could easily be forgotten. A pragmatic analysis such as the one above was easy to provide and made great sense – but this type of modern analysis rested on the claim that there was no transcendent order to which religion gave access. Most modern analyses of religion ignore the possibility of this transcendent dimension. There is generally a hidden assumption at work that no transcendent order exists and, therefore, religion becomes explainable in entirely secular terms – sociologists such as Auguste Compte rest their whole approach on this assumption.

The New Atheism

Whilst atheism has a long history with limited influence, modern atheism has risen to near dominance in the West with an accompanying erosion in the idea of any absolutes. Since atheism has been around since the dawn of philosophy, it is reasonable to question what is 'new' about the 'new atheism'. What makes it distinct from the long tradition of atheistic thinking which has been present across the centuries? There are a number of factors that contribute to the newness of approach taken by modern atheists. These include:

1. Darwinian natural selection is held to be able to produce a total and complete explanation for the existence of the diversity of the natural world as well as the existence of human beings. Dawkins argues that the hypothesis of God and hypotheses in science are similar and scientific evidence is required for both.

2. Belief in life after death is dismissed and religion is seen as a psychological prop to prevent people having to deal with the meaninglessness of the universe. Daniel Dennett, in particular, sees religion as a response to a psychological need (there are clear echoes of Sigmund Freud here).

3. Modern critiques of religion are largely based on science rather than philosophy – some of the new atheists disparage the value of philosophy when it comes to debates between religion and faith. Daniel Dennett is an exception here,

although in *The God Delusion* Dawkins makes an attempt to produce some basic philosophic arguments against God.

4. The new atheists' tone is significant. It is strident, assertive and passionate – there is an evangelical conviction in their writings that was not present in many of their predecessors.

5. The popularity of books by the new atheists is something unmatched in history. In the past, atheism was confined to a small intellectual elite and many disguised their atheism for fear of societal disapproval.

6. Morality, altruism and aesthetics are held to be explainable in psychological and sociological terms.

Whereas previous atheist offerings have been relatively individual affairs, the new atheists are much in accord and unleash a sustained and multifaceted broadside against religion. Religion is attacked not just for being false but for being positively dangerous and for being the cause of much of the suffering and of evil in the world.

The new atheists share with their older, philosophical cousins an implicit commitment to verificationism as the only way of approaching knowledge. They also, however, have a passionate conviction that their position is 'right' – there is little room for ambiguity or humility in their positions.

Led by the four celebrity atheists, sometimes known as the Four Horsemen of the Atheist Apocalypse (Daniel Dennett, Christopher Hitchens, Richard Dawkins and Sam Harris), modern atheism has become a profound influence and has established atheism as a mainstream and highly influential position. Their writings have served to lead many people to subconsciously reject the idea of God, the transcendent or any

Eternal element to human life or, at the least, to consider that a discussion of a religious perspective on life is irrelevant.

Sam Harris was born in 1967 and does not like the term atheism:

> Atheism is not a philosophy; it is not even a view of the world; it is simply a refusal to deny the obvious. Unfortunately, we live in a world in which the obvious is overlooked as a matter of principle. The obvious must be observed and re-observed and argued for. This is a thankless job. It carries with it an aura of petulance and insensitivity. It is, moreover, a job that the atheist does not want.
>
> (*Letter to a Christian Nation*)

Harris argues that no one identifies himself as a non-astrologer or a non-alchemist. Atheism is simply the noises reasonable people make when in the presence of religious dogma. In his book *The End of Faith*, he argues that religion is not simply irrational and outdated but positively dangerous:

> Our technical advances in the art of war have finally rendered our religious differences – and hence our religious beliefs – antithetical to our survival. We can no longer ignore the fact that billions of our neighbours believe in the metaphysics of martyrdom, or in the literal truth of the book of Revelation, or any of the other fantastical notions that have lurked in the minds of the faithful for millennia – because our neighbours are now armed with chemical, biological, and nuclear weapons. There is no doubt that these developments mark the terminal phase of our credulity. Words like 'God' and 'Allah' must go the way of 'Apollo' and 'Baal' or they will unmake our world.

Harris is critical of fundamentalist approaches to religion, arguing that religious texts do not stand up to scrutiny, contradict each other and often advocate behaviour that most twenty-first century people would find unacceptable. However, he extends his criticism to more moderate advocates of religion arguing that their moderate views are the result of both secular knowledge and scriptural ignorance, and that they betray both faith, by being selective about which sections of Scripture they follow, and reason, because they accept beliefs uncritically.

> The moderation we see among non-fundamentalists is not some sign that faith itself has evolved; it is, rather, the product of the many hammer blows of modernity that have exposed certain tenets of faith to doubt. Not the least among these developments has been the emergence of our tendency to value evidence and to be convinced by a proposition to the degree that there is evidence for it. Even most fundamentalists live by the lights of reason in this regard; it is just that their minds seem to have been partitioned to accommodate the profligate truth claims of their faith. Tell a devout Christian that his wife is cheating on him, or that frozen yogurt can make a man invisible, and he is likely to require as much evidence as anyone else, and to be persuaded only to the extent that you give it. Tell him that the book he keeps by his bed was written by an invisible deity who will punish him with fire for eternity if he fails to accept its every incredible claim about the universe, and he seems to require no evidence whatsoever.
>
> (Sam Harris, *The End of Faith: Religion, Terror, and the Future of Reason*)

In his 2006 book *Breaking the Spell*, Daniel Dennett argues that religion ought to be studied through the scientific lens of evolutionary biology. The "spell" that requires "breaking" is not religious belief itself but the belief that it is off-limits to or beyond scientific inquiry. He sees religion as a natural phenomenon, not a supernatural one, and argues that it is important to gain a rational understanding of it because of its influence on human beings: "I listen to all these complaints about rudeness and intemperateness, and the opinion that I come to is that there is no polite way of asking somebody: have you considered the possibility that your entire life has been devoted to a delusion? But that's a good question to ask. Of course we should ask that question and of course it's going to offend people. Tough."

Many of the new atheists have a real sense of spirituality (depending on how this term is defined). For instance Dennett, in *Breaking the Spell: Religion as a Natural Phenomenon*, says:

If you can approach the world's complexities, both its glories and its horrors, with an attitude of humble curiosity, acknowledging that however deeply you have seen, you have only scratched the surface, you will find worlds within worlds, beauties you could not heretofore imagine, and your own mundane preoccupations will shrink to proper size, not all that important in the greater scheme of things. Keeping that awestruck vision of the world ready to hand while dealing with the demands of daily living is no easy exercise, but it is definitely worth the effort, for if you can stay centred, and engaged, you will find the hard choices easier, the right words will come to you when you need them, and you will indeed be a better person. That, I propose, is the secret to spirituality, and it has nothing at all to do with believing in an immortal soul.

One of Richard Dawkins' earlier books, *The Blind Watchmaker*, refers to William Paley's argument which says that anyone finding a mechanical watch on a heath would be clear that it bears all the marks of "contrivance and design". A stone, Paley argues, might be there by chance but the complexity of a watch clearly points to an intelligence behind it, even if we did not know its purpose. Similarly, he claims that the whole of the natural world points to an intelligence behind the universe. Dawkins utterly rejects this and claims that natural selection is "blind", it has no aim, no purpose:

> Evolution has no long-term goal. There is no long-term target, no final perfection to serve as a criteria for selection... The criteria for selection is always short term, either simply survival or, more generally, reproductive success. The "watchmaker" that is cumulative natural selection is blind to the future and has no long-term goal.
> (*The Blind Watchmaker: Why the Evidence of Evolution Reveals a Universe Without Design*)

Dawkins follows Hume and describes approaches like Richard Swinburne's probability arguments for the existence of God as, "Arguments from personal incredulity." Dawkins' view is that the hypothesis of God is entirely superfluous.

In *The Selfish Gene* Dawkins claims that humans only act so that their genes may survive. All we are is mechanisms to pass on our genes in competition with other species. We are simply the mechanisms used by our genes to replicate themselves: "We are survival machines – robot vehicles blindly programmed to preserve the selfish molecules known as genes."

In *River Out of Eden* Dawkins says:

> Nature is not cruel, pitiless, indifferent. This is one of the hardest lessons for humans to learn. We cannot admit that things might be neither good nor evil, neither cruel nor kind, but simply callous – indifferent to all suffering, lacking all purpose.

Dawkins quotes Prince Philip, the Duke of Edinburgh, who, in a seminar at Windsor Castle addressed by Dr Peter Atkins, said:

> You scientists are very good at answering 'how' questions. But you must admit that you are powerless when it comes to the 'why' questions.

Dawkins rejects this – there is no why, except that anything that happens can be explained in evolutionary terms. There simply is no wider meaning or purpose. However, what science and evolution can explain are the mechanisms which bring about states of affairs.

Dawkins points out that a female digger wasp lays her larvae in the live body of a caterpillar, grasshopper or bee and ensures that its tendrils go into the nerve endings of the prey to keep it alive while it is eaten from within. To the person who recoils with horror at how a good God could allow this – Dawkins says that the question is nonsense. There is no reason – it is just an effective way of the female wasp passing on her genes.

> Now they swarm in huge colonies, safe inside gigantic lumbering robots, sealed off from the outside world, communicating with it by tortuous indirect routes, manipulating it by remote control. They are in you and me; they create us, body and mind, and their preservation is the ultimate rationale for our existence. They have come a long way, these replicators. Now they go by the name of genes and we are their survival machines.

The new atheism is so popular and so persuasive as its message is a very simple one and it easily accords with much of human experience. Science does seem to explain more and more all the time. Fewer and fewer people in the West acknowledge any sort of Eternal or transcendent dimension to life. Everyday life does seem to obey fairly clear laws based on a materialistic view of the universe. Humans are, increasingly, seen as essentially animals – the process of reproduction, for instance, is almost identical in every mammal. Sperm and egg unite to form a zygote, then an embryo and eventually live young are born which are then suckled by their mother, protected and helped to grow and develop whilst they learn to engage with the world. The process is essentially the same in a dog, cat, cow, horse, rat, mouse, giraffe, elephant, weasel, rabbit, dolphin, whale or human. The process of mourning the death of a loved one by a monkey or an elephant has remarkable parallels with human beings and can be explained in evolutionary terms. Even altruism can be shown to have an advantage and to assist in the propagation of the species and its care and continuation.

Peter Singer argues that it is necessary to confront the 'speciesism' which claims that human beings are in a distinct category from animals. All the evidence points in the opposite direction. To be sure, many animals are less conscious, less able to make choices and to act intelligently than most humans, but this does not apply to newborn babies or to humans suffering advanced dementia, Parkinson's or Huntington's diseases. What matters, argues Singer, is not species but the quality of life. Countless thousands of dogs, cats, horses and other animals are put out of their misery when they are suffering and we should be willing to extend the same compassion to, for instance, an unwanted full-term baby that is badly disabled and whose prospect of any real quality of life would be poor. Better, Singer argues, to kill the unwanted baby and to have another one whose quality of life would be better. Singer argues that the idea that human life is sacred is medieval and based on Judaism, Christianity and Islam. In a world where belief in God is widely dismissed, the idea that human life is sacred just because it is human should be rejected. Just as Copernicus and Galileo showed that the earth was not flat and went round the sun, so today the time has come to accept that it is simply no longer tenable to hold that human life is sacred.

Singer argued, in an article in the British journal *The Spectator* in 1995, that he and the then Pope at least clearly know what is at stake – the issue is Sanctity of Life which the Pope affirms and Peter Singer rejects.

The religious imperative which held sway over the Western world has largely died – increasingly religion or interest in it has become a marginal activity and is no longer seen as standing for absolute Truth or an Eternal dimension to reality. Sociology, psychology, anthropology are all important disciplines, but they are, when applied to religion, essentially reductionist. Closet verificationism (in other words undeclared verificationism) holds sway and most people have lost interest in any search for absolute Truth. Atheism, as we have seen, has contributed to this. It is part of the aim of this book to question the validity of the verificationist and materialist assumptions and to argue that consideration of absolute Truth means going beyond empirical evidence and seeking an understanding both of reality and of Truth in a different way.

Chapter Four

A Post Truth World

Increasingly, fame is a commodity that is prized for itself alone. It does not matter what a person is famous for, the point is to be famous. The number of 'hits', 'likes' or 'friends' on social media is, for some, directly related to their feeling of self-worth. YouTube has convinced every person that they have a voice as well as a set of opinions that need to be heard and respected. In many schools teachers are told that they must value every opinion no matter how lacking in argument or evidence, and young people are brought up to value celebrity and popularity. The person with few 'followers' is a loser. Social media rewards 'takedowns' of people. The more famous the person measured (in terms of number of followers) that can be challenged and brought down, the brighter shines the star of the person who has carried out the action and, of course, the more followers they will have on Facebook and Twitter. In 2016 when Britain voted to leave the European Union, the BBC felt forced to give equal weight to views on both sides without challenging or questioning statements or assumptions that were blatantly false in case they were accused of bias. In the United States, Donald Trump rejected the reports from dispassionate media and instead uses powerful media outlets (such as Fox News) allied to him to propagate 'alternative facts' which were congenial to his 'base' supporters. The death of truth has profound significance.

In Britain in 2017, a survey of 24 to 35 year olds disclosed that two out of three had no religion at all and this carried with it a lack of interest in any search for ultimate Truth since truth becomes simply what has been constructed by human beings. These young people are part of the post-truth generation and their numbers are certain to rise. Steve Turner's poem "Creed" represents the modern position well.

Since the dawn of time, human beings have sought Truth. Mystics sought it in silence and in the stars, warriors sought it in war, artists sought to convey it on the walls of caves or on parchment, writers sought to record it, great rulers sought to immortalize it in stone, some sought to live it whilst others fled from it in fear. However, no one seriously doubted that Truth was there – amorphous, multifaceted, always elusive, always 'other', always partial and incomplete. Few doubted the existence of Truth – it was the lodestar of the wise and the rapture of the foolish. Philosophers sought it and sometimes thought they had found it but it escaped from their definitions and remained out of reach, refusing to be defined or confined, refusing to conform to the categories that sought to cage it.

There is a moral dimension to the study of issues of truth and knowledge. There have been periods in history when scepticism was rampant, and in these periods a whole way of life and morality was called into question. Once the process of questioning what we know seriously begins, it gives rise to a moral uneasiness. Two examples will illustrate this.

The Greek philosopher Protagoras' claim that "man is the measure of all things" was a position of scepticism whereby human perception of reality was the final arbiter of certainty. Out of the relativism that this implied arose Plato's writings on moral issues, particularly Plato's *Theaetetus* in which he portrays Socrates expressing admiration for the wisdom of Protagoras whilst not agreeing with him. Socrates and Plato sought to separate knowledge from mere opinion. Knowledge, for Plato, was concerned with the timeless and spaceless Forms which were neither creative nor did they create. The Forms were organised so that the highest Form was the Form of the Good, and knowledge and morality were, therefore, closely related. For Plato, to act badly was due to ignorance and his views left no space for someone knowing what was wrong yet choosing to do this nevertheless. Plato's strongly-held realist views on the nature of reality came out of a background influenced by the relativism of Protagoras.

The period leading up to Descartes was an era when people came to disagree about the religious truths which previously had been held as certain – there was, therefore, a moral uneasiness similar to that before Plato. The Church as a source for absolute truth claims was substituted, through Luther and other reformers, by the authority of conscience and appeal to the Bible. The certainties of the old order gave way, following Luther's challenges, to the methodological doubts of Descartes and the attempt to find something that could be known for certain and which could provide a foundation for claims to knowledge. Following the Reformation and the Enlightenment people no longer knew where they stood, and Descartes sought to provide a firm underpinning for claims to knowledge.

In both these periods scepticism was commonly accepted and this was not isolated from a general unease in society. We have the same problem today where there is a general scepticism coupled with a recognition that Western society has lost its way and has no clear ideas of the values for which it stands or, indeed, if it stands for anything. When Eastern Europe fell to capitalism, it brought supposed benefits such as freedom but it also brought the lack of values that have become widely accepted in Western society. Freedom in Eastern Europe was initially at least bought at a heavy price including high unemployment, lack of food in some areas, the absence of leisure facilities that were generally accepted under the communist regime, a feeling of hopelessness and a massive increase in corruption. A small elite at the apex of society prospered hugely, but for the rest the advantages of 'freedom' have been mitigated by many adverse factors. It is not surprising that in parts of Russia and some of the former Soviet satellites there is a yearning for the old days with their clearly laid down certainties when at least there was food and employment, and the Soviet Union was respected around the world as a superpower. These issues are rarely confronted today since Western interest in values, as in truth, is now peripheral, yet to many round the world who suffer because of the acceptance of Western 'values' that have been imposed on them, the issues of the ends towards which society is directed are real. Whereas 'The West' once considered it stood for profound ideas such as freedom, democracy, justice and human rights, today it is seen by many to be dominated by money, power and self-interest. Since truth has disappeared, so have many of the values for which it traditionally stood.

Investigations of knowledge and truth are not self-contained. They affect the whole of a society and the way society sees itself and conducts itself. They affect moral issues from sexuality to business, from fossil fuels to the commercial exploitation of children. Understanding the moral uneasiness of society is part of understanding scepticism. This is a preliminary point but one whose significance will emerge later.

The post-truth world that we live in asserts that Truth (with a capital 'T') is dead. We live in a world of multiple narratives where absolutes are widely derided. The idea of any 'meta-narrative', any overarching truth which would make some sense of the human condition is rejected. The multiple claims by different religions and sects, the multiple narratives of different media, the influences of sex, gender and culture as well as the inevitably partial nature of history and even our decreasing knowledge of the total of reality (whatever we take this to be) makes the search for Truth seem to be folly. Instead of science advancing towards greater and greater understanding of 'reality', our constantly increasing scientific knowledge serves to demonstrate just how little we know. At the end of the nineteenth century most physicists thought that science was on the verge of being able to explain all reality. Such a dream is now a distant memory. Whether in terms of the increasingly elusive dark matter or the relationship between the apparent randomness and chaos of reality at the Planck scale combined with order at the human scale, we know less and less about more and more.

Philosophers from ancient times have been preoccupied with the search for Absolute Truth – indeed this was the goal of most philosophers across the centuries. The subject of epistemology is precisely concerned to seek the foundations for knowledge. But the different approaches have yielded even greater uncertainty. Traditionally there was a search for absolute foundations for knowledge whether these depended on experience (Aristotle, Locke and the empiricist tradition) or Mathematics (Plato, Descartes and the rationalists) but no one really denied that foundations for knowledge existed – except for an ever-present minority of sceptics who always rejected the human ability to arrive at absolute truth. In the past, almost everyone was a philosophic 'realist'.

A realist maintains that a statement is either true or false depending on whether or not it corresponds or refers to the state of affairs which it purports to describe. Thus 'There is water in that glass' would be true iff (if and only if) there is, indeed, water in the glass to which reference is made. 'There are yellow spiders on Mars' is true iff there are, in fact, yellow spiders on Mars. It is important to recognise that truth on this understanding does not depend on evidence but on the state of affairs being described. We have no idea whether there are or could be yellow spiders on Mars, but the realist will claim that this is either true or false depending on the state of affairs on Mars. Lack of evidence or proof is not the same as lack of truth.

The trouble is that since the work of GE Moore (in "In Defence of Common Sense", 1925) the idea of absolute foundations for knowledge has largely been rejected. Instead (as Ludwig Wittgenstein showed when discussing Moore's paper in his lectures which were collected together into a book by his students entitled *On Certainty* – published in 1969 posthumously) human beings are educated into what he calls a "form of life", possibly better expressed as a frame of reference, which everyone in their culture accepts and which provides the foundations of knowledge claims within their different cultures and frames of reference.

Wittgenstein agreed with Moore's analysis except on one crucial point. Moore argued that doubt about these banal statements did not make sense and that they were true. Wittgenstein agreed on the first of these and not the second. Doubt about them is, indeed, impossible, but the issue of truth is more complex. We cannot know they are true in any realist sense. Describing a particular part of the spectrum as 'yellow' is not objectively true – it is true within a particular form of reference. In English 'chair' refers to the piece of furniture on which we sit, but Romans had no word for 'chair' since they used couches. Language is dynamic, meanings change. In the early part of the twentieth century, the word 'gay' referred to a happy individual, now it is generally used to refer to someone who is homosexual or lesbian. 'Wicked' was used to refer to something that was terrible and wrong. In some Western cultures today it is used to indicate something that is 'cool'. 'Marriage' used to refer to a union of a man and a woman, today in many societies it can refer to same sex marriages and there are even beginning to be suggestions that the term should also be applied to relationships between a human and an intelligent cyborg or AI. The idea of fixed meanings has passed, we are in a world of fluidity. Meaning thus depends on the way that words are used in a particular society. In the US cars have hoods and trunks, in the UK, Australia and New Zealand they have bonnets and boots.

This gives rise to 'anti-realism' (sometimes referred to as non-realism) in which truth depends on coherence: On what is accepted as true within a particular form of life. Truth, then, becomes dependent on the frame of reference one inhabits and the idea of any single, absolute frame of reference is dismissed. Every individual is educated by their parents from a very early age into seeing the world in a particular way. They are taught language and the basic vocabulary of any child – this basic vocabulary represents the foundations of their frame of reference. This can be illustrated by any child of five who may ask, "Why, Mummy?" Mummy will answer more or less patiently, but if the 'Why' questions continue then there comes a point when answers come to an end. There is no longer any justification.

> "Why do we need chairs, Mummy?" ... "Because we need to be able to sit down somewhere."
> "Why do we need to sit down, Mummy?" ... "Because it is more restful to sit down sometimes and it helps to sit down to do drawing or to eat our food."
> "Why is this called a chair, Mummy?" ... "It just is... now go and play."

There comes a point when the regress of explanation stops. 'Mummy' has to say: "This is just the way it is, this is just what we do." GE Moore argued that instead of language making contact with the world with certain indubitable statements that can be proved to be true (for instance the claims of sense experience or mathematics), there comes a point when it simply no longer makes sense to ask questions. If someone really asks justification for:

> This is yellow.
> This is a window.
> This is a chair.
> There is a human body that is my human body.

then either they need to learn English, or they are mentally ill – or they are doing philosophy. Some questions are so banal, so basic that doubt about them is not possible. They are the ground rules of our form of life or frame of reference and we were taught these ground rules when we first learnt language at our parents' knees.

This is significant as if truth depends on what is agreed within a culture, as the anti-realists claim, then truth is radically perspectival. In religious terms this can be very challenging. Take the following core statements that lie at the heart of Judaism, Christianity and Islam:

1. God promised much of the land of Palestine to the people of Israel in perpetuity.
2. Jesus died on the cross and rose on the third day.
3. There is one God who is Allah, and Muhammad is His prophet.

Every Jew, Christian and Muslim will agree that, respectively, statements (1), (2) and (3) are true but what this means is now claimed to be different. The realist will say that these statements are true or false because they correspond to the actual event. Either Jesus did die on the cross and rose on the third day or he did not. The Muslim will say that either Muhammad was the prophet of God or he was not. The anti-realist will reject this and will instead say that these statements are unequivocally true within the different forms of life or frames of reference of the Jew, Christian or Muslim. There is no absolute truth – or at least none that anyone can know. All that can be said is that these statements are regarded as unquestionably true or false within different religious forms of life. (2) is true within Christianity, not within Judaism and Islam. (1) is true within Judaism (at least in many forms of Orthodox Judaism) but not in Christianity or Islam.

It is vital to recognise that when the Jew says that God promised certain land to the people of Israel and when the Muslim said that

God did not, they are not, on the anti-realist view, contradicting each other. Both are making true statements from within their different frames of references. Truth, then, depends on culture and the frame of reference one inhabits. Children are educated into their parents' form of life or frame of reference, and the basic axioms of this form of life are unquestioned – at least until the child grows to an adult and, even then, any questioning is likely to be uncomfortable. To say to a faithful Muslim that perhaps Muhammad wrote the Qur'an rather than having it dictated by the Archangel would be incredibly offensive and might provoke a violent response as it strikes at the heart of the form of life of the Islamic community. This is why so many countries have laws against blasphemy as such strong emotions arise when basic assumptions are questioned or challenged.

The same can apply to science. Before Copernicus and Galileo everyone agreed that the earth was at the centre of the universe. Everyone agreed that the stars and plants moved in circular or elliptical orbits around the earth. This was truth. Everyone accepted it and, the anti-realist says, this made it true. After Newton, everyone accepted that the universe was like a great machine. Everyone agreed that the stars, the planets and everything on earth obeyed clear causal laws – like a great watch. Everyone accepted that, given limited time, science would be able to provide a complete explanation of reality. At the end of the 19th century, many scientists could see science coming to an end because a total explanation would be found. This was truth. It was accepted by all the greatest scientists at all the best universities. The universe was made up of matter and matter obeyed causal laws. Everyone agreed and this made it true – at least on the anti-realist view. The brain was like an advanced computer and one could explain consciousness and human behaviour in essentially causal ways. We still have this latter view today in evolutionary psychology which promises a complete explanation for all human behaviour, and the majority of the world's population regard matter as primary. This whole picture was and, largely, is true because everyone accepted it.

Until along come Einstein, Schrödinger, Bohr and others and show that this whole picture is radically inadequate. At the most basic level of reality there is no matter, there are not even electrons – there are potential electrons. Consciousness is vastly more complex than we can imagine and most certainly not explainable just in terms of the behaviour of neurons in the brain. Gradually (all too slowly) the old paradigm is breaking down and (all too slowly) a new one emerges which, in its turn, will be true because that is what everyone accepts.

It was the great philosopher of science, Thomas Kuhn, who showed that science operates within a paradigm that everyone agrees upon and that is regarded as true, until the paradigm breaks down and a new one emerges.

In every field of human endeavour and even in the most mundane areas of life, truth has come to be seen to be dependent on culture, on perspective and on the frame of reference one inhabits. The days of certainty and any claim to absolute Truth (note the capital) seem to be past.

Modernism is not modern. It is the term given to that period in which human reason became autonomous and no longer dependent on metaphysics or religion. It is generally dated from around the Enlightenment and it began the period of the confidence of human beings in their ability to understand the world of which they are a part. Human beings became independent and, the Enlightenment, as Kant put it, represented "man's release from his self-incurred tutelage". Human beings became self-sufficient and did not need to rely on revelation and hence, by implication, entered the modern world. Three figures, in particular, stand out at the advent of the modern world – Nicolaus Copernicus (1473–1543) showed that the earth revolved around the sun challenging the idea that this world was the centre of the Universe; Galileo Galilei (1564–1642) used telescopes to understand the movement of the stars; and Isaac Newton (1642–1727) discovered the force of gravitation. The universe suddenly seemed accessible to human reason and, although faith in God remained, God's role seemed much reduced since natural forces could explain nearly all observed movements. Descartes (1596–1650), with his emphasis on the inner self, also helped in a reorientation which placed human beings in a position to understand the world, and mathematics and science seemed to provide the tools by which this might be achieved.

Two great cross currents in Western thoughts and ideas have come together to bring us to the Post-modern predicament:

1. The first is the Enlightenment with its faith in human reason and the scientific enterprise. The success of science and its achievements is undisputed, but by explaining nearly everything it comes close to explaining nothing. Human beings are their genes, we are lonely accidents of the evolutionary process in a small planet of a minor star in one of a billion galaxies. We are insignificant flotsam who exist for no reason and no purpose but who can, through science, increasingly understand facts about what we are.

2. On the other side stands the Romantic movement stemming from figures such as Walt Whitman, Coleridge, Wordsworth and Goethe who resisted the scientific advances and wished to see human beings as an integral part of nature and who appeal to a spiritual understanding of reality that cannot be captured by the scientist. Romanticism appeals to the individual to overcome his or her conditioning and to find meaning in love, art and beauty – it places a high stress on the individual and gives birth, in the twentieth century, to existentialist philosophy.

These two currents have profoundly influenced us today and many of us live in both these two worlds – but integrating them is far from easy. Out of the tension between these two powerful streams in Western thoughts, both confident, both highly influential, both assertive, emerges postmodernism. To understand its relevance today we have to return to the beginning of the nineteenth century.

Nietzsche was born on 15th October 1844; he was the son of devout Lutheran parents yet he was an implacable foe of Christianity. He always discouraged convinced Christians from reading his books because he realised the effect they would have. When Nietzsche says that, "God is dead," he is not rejecting the God of traditional Christianity, Islam and Judaism in the way that an atheist might. Instead he is rejecting a way of looking at the world and the possibility of a God's eye view, of some absolute perspective from which the world can be viewed. With the death of God, it is claimed, goes the death of all the Platonic and absolute values. God dies, and so do metaphysics, Truth, Goodness, Justice and Virtue. The goal of seeking some absolute Truth is, according to Nietzsche, as dead and as futile as God. What, then, is truth? According to Nietzsche it is:

A mobile army of metaphors, metonymies, anthropomorphisms: in short a sum of human relations which become poetically and rhetorically intensified, metamorphosed, adorned and after a long usage seem to a nation fixed, canonic, binding; truths are illusions of which one has forgotten that they are illusions.

(*On Truth and Lies in a Nonmoral Sense*, 1879)

A human being does not discover truths, rather he:

... always discovered in things only that which he had put into them!

For Nietzsche morality itself is a sign of decadence because it is holding on to the view that there are such things as values, virtues and good and evil. No such things exist except in so far as we have created them and "God is dead," he claimed, because human beings now recognise God as something we have generated to respond to our needs. With this recognition, all those things which the word God stood for such as absolute value and truth die as well. For Nietzsche, his superman ('overman') moves beyond good and evil as categories that no longer have meaning. His work, if it is accepted, marks the end of an era of metaphysical enquiry. There is no ready-made world which we discover, no essential nature of a thing as Aristotle thought – there is only our own perspective. Human beings are on their own with no landmarks to guide them in a sea of relativity. They can now become gods if they will throw off the trappings of convention which seek to shackle and constrain them with now discredited modes of thinking.

Nietzsche did not consider that life had any aim or point to be discovered in some way – except that he considered that exceptional human beings have to come to the state where they can give life a purpose or aim. For Nietzsche, the aim of all human existence is the production of the Superman, the man with a will to power. This is almost an evolutionary step for human beings to move to become a new and higher level person beyond the herd.

This is, of course, a highly elitist view and the common mass of human beings is needed as a means to the end of the emergence of the higher individual. Effectively Nietzsche considered slavery to be the basis of culture – it is out of slavery that the higher individual can emerge. In *The Dawn of Day*, Nietzsche admits that some will have to do the boring, rough and dirty work of society in order that the higher level individuals may emerge. There is truth in this – thus the brilliance of Greek philosophy was only possible because of the leisure afforded to a narrow range of people by the work of slaves. The great art of the middle ages was possible only because of the labour and suffering of untold thousands who worked to create the wealth and to build the cathedrals that enabled the art to be created.

Nietzsche condemns and warns of the dangers of journalism – this is the means of expression as well as the way of forming the thinking of the herd of ordinary people who never read anything beyond tabloid newspapers and whose views can, therefore, be formed and moulded with great ease. Even those who consider themselves wise generally are dominated by the media and they will often choose to only read or listen to the views of those organs which pander to and confirm their own prejudices.

As he writes:

Depart not hence, but read what Greek folk-wisdom says of this same life, which with such inexplicable cheerfulness spreads out before thee. There is an ancient story that King Midas hunted in the forest a long time for the wise Silenus, the companion of Dionysius, without capturing him. When at last he fell into his hands, the king asked what was best of all and most desirable for man. Fixed and immovable, the demon remained silent; till at last, forced by the king, he broke out with shrill laughter into these words: "Oh wretched race of a day, children of chance and misery, why do ye compel me to say to you what is most expedient for you not to hear? What is best of all is for ever beyond your reach, not to be born, not to be, to be nothing. The second best for you, however, is soon to die."

(*The Birth of Tragedy*)

As the great Jesuit philosopher Frederick Copleston says, this pessimism leaves only two possible paths open:

One is to create a dream world, an artistically optimistic world

– and this is the Apollonian way: the other is to face the real nature of the world and affirm it, accept it, say "yes" to it – this is the Dionysian way. The Apollonian way is represented in the Olympian religion.

The alternatives are simple, and they face us just as much today once we accept that the world is meaningless – either create an optimistic view of the world based on a transcendent order and an assumption of God or gods or of some absolute morality, or else face the meaninglessness of the world as it really is and to relish this, to live with this with full joy and acceptance. The latter is the way of Dionysius which Nietzsche applauds. The Dionysian way recognises the meaningless and purposelessness of life as it is, but does not sink into pessimism – it says an emphatic 'yes' to all of life. As Nietzsche says:

It is the final, cheerfullest, exuberantly mad-and-merriest Yes to life.

This is the way of the strong individual who is not taken in by illusion. Any such strong person will need courage and strength, the courage and strength to live by his own light, to create meaning where none exists and, above all, not to be dragged down by the crowd. Nietzsche has nothing but contempt for the crowd or the herd as he sometimes refers to the mass of human beings. Nietzsche believed that the Will to Power exists everywhere and the herd exerts a Will to Power over the noble and strong man – who must therefore resist. The weak try to drag down the strong and do so by force of numbers, by public opinion, and destroy the strong by the power of mediocrity.

The very attempt to persuade another to one's own perspective is an exercise in power. Nietzsche, as we have seen, maintained that the use and abuse of power was a feature of all humanity. Even those who sought to supposedly help others were thereby exercising a form of dominion over them. The will to power of one human being over another or of one society over another is endemic in the human condition and the 'superman' is the one who will refuse to be thus dominated and subjugated, and who chooses his own path. Totalitarianism and power can be seen to go hand in hand – Nietzsche is sometimes described as the philosopher of the German Nazis, but this is to radically misunderstand him. The Nazis developed an extreme, totalitarian system which Nietzsche would have rejected out of hand. When Nietzsche's madman confronts the crowd in the marketplace and proclaims that, "God is dead... We have killed him you and I," the madman goes on to ask:

> Is not the greatness of this deed too much for us? Must not we ourselves become gods simply to seem worthy of it? There has never been a greater deed – and whosoever shall be born after us, for the sake of this deed, shall be part of a great humanity than all history.
>
> ("The Parable of the Madman", 1882)

The death of God opens the way for the 'overman' ('Ubermensch' – sometimes misleadingly translated into English as the 'superman'), the man who throws aside all the trappings of convention and imposed world-views and thereby affects humanity down the centuries. As Feuerbach realised, man has, in becoming the measure of all things, also become God and Habermas sees Nietzsche as marking the advent of postmodernity.

There is no clear moment when postmodernism began just as there is no clear definition of what it is. The term postmodernism was first coined by Arnold Toynbee in the late 1930s but it is a particular phenomenon of French culture with its passion for French language and the power of texts – some, therefore, see its origins as lying in the student riots in Paris in 1968 and the

Marxist and anarchist sentiments that lay beneath French culture at the time. To the postmodern mind, context and perspective are everything and the reality we talk about and inhabit is one that we construct, radically alterable and with no fixed points.

There are no absolutes, no rocks of certainty from which one can stand firm outside the constant sea of change – we are imbedded in these tossing and raging waters, and reality is the reality seen from our particular point within it. The most we can achieve is to, by great effort, understand another's perspective whilst recognising that he or she is also immersed in the constant waters of change, but his or her perspective is no more privileged than ours. The search for certainty or for any rock to cling to is folly and Truth (at least with a capital 'T') has become a dirty word, a word used only by those who have failed to appreciate the human condition and who are embedded in a world-view which is considered discredited. As Nietzsche puts it:

... facts are precisely what there is not, only interpretations.

The attempt by Western society to impose a global hegemony (by vehicles such as capitalism, the World Bank, global satellite links, advertising and a single world economic order etc.) is precisely the sort of exercise in dominance that postmodernism rejects. This is a rejection of the diversity; the radical relativism and the emphasis on difference that are postmodernism's central affirmations.

The same would, of course, be true for any alternative system (for instance Islam) which claimed that it had the 'right' answer and which attempted to impose its beliefs – although it is, perhaps, significant that postmodernism shows its own hidden agenda by not attacking such systems with anything like the attention or focus reserved for the Western tradition.

Deconstructionism and postmodernism go hand in hand. For someone to claim that there is a 'postmodern view of the world' almost amounts to a contradiction, as the most that might be said is that there is no single view of the world. The postmodernist rejects any idea of good art, as of beauty and of truth – we are children of a sea of flux and now that God has been rejected as an underpinning of beauty, art, culture and truth, there is no authenticity.

With postmodernism, the end of the road has arrived. Philosophy, theology, art, music, literature and indeed science are all folly. The most they can do is to shock us out of complacency, to force us to break free from the bounds of our conditioning, to see the world differently. (Although not, of course, in any better way. There is no idea of progress, of having advanced.) In a way, postmodernism is a logical outworking of Darwinian evolution. Just as the survival of the fittest holds that 'whatever is, is right', so the same applies in all other fields as well as in biology. The confidence to be found in science in the seventeenth and eighteenth centuries and amongst the Romantics of the nineteenth century has vanished. As Dostoyevsky's Ivan Karamazov says, with the death of God "all is permitted". There is no wrong and no right – there is simply what we have in existence. Camus, in his novels such as *The Plague* and *The Fall*, tried to understand how Ivan's rebellion against God in the name of humanity could have ended in Stalin, Hitler and Pol Pot's death camps. The answer is, of course, that if everything is indeed permitted, if morality has no grounds, if there are no values then there is no ground to condemn such atrocities except from within one's own culture. On this basis, those defendants at the Nuremberg Trials who claimed that the trials were just the morality of the victors judging those of the vanquished were right. The prosecutors, of course, claimed that this was not the case – but they were working with an Aristotelian form of morality grounded in a common human nature which postmodernists would certainly reject.

Richard Tarnas expresses it well:

The situation recognized by John Dewey (1859–1952) at the start of the century, that "despair of any integrated outlook and attitude [is] the chief intellectual characteristic of the present age," has been enshrined as the essence of the postmodern vision, as in Jean-François Lyotard's definition of postmodern as "incredulity toward metanarratives." Here, paradoxically, we can recognize something of the old confidence of the modern mind in the superiority of its own perspective. Only whereas the modern mind's conviction of superiority derived from its awareness of possessing in an absolute sense more knowledge than its predecessors, the postmodern mind's sense of superiority derives from its special awareness of how little knowledge can be claimed by any mind, itself included.

(*The Passion of the Western Mind*)

Graham Ward describes surfing the net as the ultimate postmodern experience. As individuals sit at their computer consoles, they can not only access but also construct a reality which can be in contact, simultaneously, with almost anywhere in the world. Most net identities are fictitious and the images that are seen are often virtual images. Time disappears and there is a constant and ever-changing flow of information. Virtual reality computer games – still in their infancy – enable people to inhabit the world in which they play – to sunbathe on tropical islands, to make love to beautiful women or men, to take part in intergalactic wars and to meet and to destroy, love or befriend virtual people. Cyberspace is real, it exists and we can access it – tomorrow we may be able to live in it – it is a reality that we construct or that is constructed for us by others. We are entering an era where we can live in the dreams of our own creation, we can make love to the man or woman of our choice, journey to the far side of Jupiter, visit the wilds of the Amazon or climb Mt Everest, party with friends – and all without leaving the solitude of our living room and computer terminal.

Postmodernism claims a position of superiority from which it rejects all the hard striving of philosophy and any idea of a search for truth. It makes seriousness in living and seriousness about truth to be something to be derided – ideas whose time has passed and which are not worthy of serious discussion. This is, I want to argue, a radically mistaken attitude.

Postmodernism can be seen as Cartesian doubt carried to its extreme – everything is doubted, but not because there might be a true reality to which we are not sure we have access. There is no such reality; there is only our radically contingent perspective. It is possible to isolate some principles which underpin the postmodernist positions, although there is no single position that may be regarded as 'the' postmodern position. The whole enterprise is vague, diffuse and complex and resists easy categorisation. However, broadly, the essential elements include the following:

1. Reality is a product of constant change and flux, there are no fixed certainties.
2. Human beings are not apart from this reality and there is no one reality, instead reality itself is ever changing.
3. Abstract principles, metaphysics and any search for Truth or for any commitment to an ontology independent of our experience are to be rejected.
4. There are, and can be, no final truths nor is there any possible idea of progress.
5. Gender differences are of vital importance in forming and interpreting reality. For too long, reality has been and is constructed on male terms and this has been and is used as a vehicle for oppression.
6. There needs to be greater emphasis on difference and a rejection of any idea of a single nature. Male, patriarchal, Western ideas and values deny difference and attempt to

impose an artificial uniformity.

7. In art, science, aesthetics, literature, morality and religion as well as in any other field, there are no absolutes. (At Harvard University, English students insisted that the Boston telephone directory should be placed on the reading list alongside the works of Shakespeare as, to the postmodern mind, the one has no more intrinsic value than the other, just as a child's painting daub has no more value than a Picasso or a Constable or the music of a punk band than Mozart.)

Each of these statements can be challenged and each can be shown to be at least legitimately debatable. For instance, the gender bias idea is a strong argument – clearly an awful lot of history and culture has ignored the perspective and influence of women. However, this is not to say there are no common human values. It is true that diversity has been under-recognised and that some values have been used to oppress others. However, this is a much more modest claim than most postmodernists are making. Of course, human beings vary widely and it is right to recognise these differences. Some are musicians, some sports women, some artists, some good with their hands – but some are also psychopaths and some abusers of young children. We need to be able to say that in the latter cases there is something wrong with the individuals in question, that they need help and that their full human potential is not being realised.

The apparently plausible assertion that in art, science, aesthetics, literature, morality and religion as well as in any other field there are no absolutes is problematic because of the word 'absolute'. Plato was an absolutist – he believed that the Forms of Beauty, Truth, Justice and the Good existed timelessly and spacelessly, and that examples of beauty, truth, justice and goodness in some ways participated or shared in this absolute reality. It may be that, for instance, beauty is culturally relative

– certainly the appreciation of the beauty of the human female form varies widely between different cultures. Nevertheless, the fact that examples of cultural relativity can be cited does not necessarily mean that in all the categories set out above there are no absolutes. At most it may mark the beginning of what would have to be a detailed discussion of whether, in any of the areas listed, there are any absolute truths to be known. There may be – or there may not be, but the issue is open. A three-year-old child may daub some paint on a piece of paper, but to claim that there is no intrinsic difference in quality between this and the work of a Constable or a Turner seems to be simply perverse.

The encyclical *Fides et Ratio* (1998) was arguably the most important of Pope John Paul II's pontificate, and the issues it raised were placed by Pope Benedict XVI at the heart of his period of office. The document deals with the issue of Truth and the decline in importance of Truth in modern society as well as the relationship between faith and reason. Pope Benedict identified the issue of Truth as the single most important issue facing the world today.

The encyclical strongly endorses the importance of philosophy and also reason. It affirms the importance of philosophy as an autonomous discipline which is vital to engage with a postmodern world. It bemoans the lack of concern with truth and sees much of modern philosophy as having become preoccupied with linguistic analysis and having lost sight of the importance of the traditional role of philosophy – which included a search for wisdom, the attempt to understand purpose and meaning. Everything, it claims, is reduced to opinion:

This has given rise to different forms of agnosticism and relativism which have led philosophical research to lose its way in the shifting sands of widespread scepticism.

Recent times have seen the rise to prominence of various

doctrines which tend to devalue even the truths which had been judged certain.

A legitimate plurality of positions has yielded to an undifferentiated pluralism, based upon the assumption that all positions are equally valid, which is one of today's most widespread symptoms of the lack of confidence in truth.

People rest content with partial and provisional truths, no longer seeking to ask radical questions about the meaning and ultimate foundation of human, personal and social existence.

With its enduring appeal to the search for truth, philosophy has the great responsibility of forming thought and culture; and now it must strive resolutely to recover its original vocation.

The document argues that:

... a positivistic mentality took hold which not only abandoned the Christian vision of the world, but more especially rejected every appeal to a metaphysical or moral vision.
(This was a reference to AJ Ayer and the logical positivists.)

It follows that certain scientists, lacking any ethical point of reference, are in danger of putting at the centre of their concerns something other than the human person and the entirety of the person's life.

As a result of the crisis of rationalism, what has appeared finally is nihilism.

As a philosophy of nothingness, (Nihilism) has a certain attraction for people of our time. ... Its adherents claim that the search is an end in itself, without any hope or possibility of ever attaining the goal of truth. In the nihilist interpretation, life is no more than an occasion for sensations and experiences in which the ephemeral has pride of place. Nihilism is at the root of the widespread mentality which claims that a definitive commitment should no longer be made, because everything is fleeting and provisional.

The encyclical strongly endorses the importance of philosophy but warns that:

> … the role of philosophy itself has changed in modern culture. From universal wisdom and learning, it has been gradually reduced to one of the many fields of human knowing; indeed in some ways it has been consigned to a wholly marginal role. Other forms of rationality have acquired an ever higher profile, making philosophical learning appear all the more peripheral. These forms of rationality are directed not towards the contemplation of truth and the search for the ultimate goal and meaning of life; but instead, as 'instrumental reason', they are directed – actually or potentially – towards the promotion of utilitarian ends, towards enjoyment or power.

> In the wake of these cultural shifts, some philosophers have abandoned the search for truth in itself and made their sole aim the attainment of a subjective certainty or a pragmatic sense of utility.

> This rapid survey of the history of philosophy, then, reveals a growing separation between faith and philosophical reason… closer scrutiny shows that even in the philosophical thinking of those who helped drive faith and reason further apart there are found at times precious and seminal insights which, if pursued and developed with mind and heart rightly tuned,

can lead to the discovery of truth's way.

Such insights are found, for instance, in penetrating analyses of perception and experience, of the imaginary and the unconscious, of personhood and intersubjectivity, of freedom and values, of time and history. The theme of death as well can become for all thinkers an incisive appeal to seek within themselves the true meaning of their own life.

Pope John Paul II made the following appeal:

This is why I make this strong and insistent appeal – not, I trust, untimely – that faith and philosophy recover the profound unity which allows them to stand in harmony with their nature without compromising their mutual autonomy.

Socrates, one of the greatest ever philosophers, delighted in speaking to 16 to 18 year olds whose minds were open and were not yet ossified and closed by culture, convention and 'accepted values'. This was not acceptable to the middle class citizens of Athens who put him on trial for atheism (because he did not believe in the state gods) and 'corrupting the young' because he wanted young people to think for themselves independently of the agenda of the rich and powerful, against their parents who wanted young people to conform to their way of thinking. Parents seek to impose their own truth, sometimes seeking to live their own lives again through their children and, above all, not wanting to see their own view of the world challenged. Seeking absolute truth is subversive, it challenges contemporary culture and contemporary ways of thinking, and this is the last thing most parents want. They want their children to grow up thinking as they do, aspiring to the same values that they have, thinking the same things are right and wrong, good and evil. They want conformity. That is why the search for Truth is seditious, challenging and generally unpopular as it questions the conventional orthodoxy of society.

For Plato (p. 17) we live in a shadow world and we see temporal and spatial approximations of the absolute, Eternal ideas of the Good, the Beautiful and the True – but the modern world rejects any such ideas, and sees goodness, beauty and truth as entirely relative to culture. The idea of absolutes is, so it is claimed, past; and instead of seeking Truth, artists and musicians seek to show the transitory, ephemeral nature of reality itself..

Chapter Five

Artificial Intelligence and the Future of Humanity

The near collapse in the importance of Truth is linked to a lack of interest in what it means to be human. Increasingly human beings are defined in economic and behaviourist terms. As we have seen, the boundaries between humans and animals are progressively challenged (p. 48) and education is increasingly concerned to produce workers who can be efficient and contribute to the good of the society which is largely measured in financial terms. This lack of interest in what it means to be human is accentuated by the rise of Artificial Intelligence.

Artificial intelligence is developing with incredible rapidity. Raymond Kurzweil predicted that the processing power of computers would double every two years and whilst there is some doubt whether this rate of increase can be maintained, there is no question that there has been exponential growth. Advanced artificial intelligence is just round the corner and provides enormous opportunities, prospective benefits and very real challenges. The world is going to be changed in a way that very few people comprehend and that is rarely discussed in government circles. The consequences are momentous and profound. What has this to do with the issue of truth? The answer is a great deal because it relates directly to the question of what it means to be human, and to any possible distinction between human beings, animals and artificial intelligence.

China is in the forefront of developments in advanced AI and is using it in an unprecedented way to monitor its own population. They now have adopted a ubiquitous "reputation rating" which will enable the government to monitor every individual for social conformity and to penalize those who do not conform. Those who have a low score will be unable to buy air or train tickets and will be marginalised by society. They will lose whatever freedom they have, and will have to conform or face tremendous economic and possibly penal consequences. The effects of this constant monitoring of every aspect of daily life will effectively lead to a new form of slavery and orthodoxy, and the Chinese model is already being introduced by other countries with authoritarian regimes. Even in democracies people will be encouraged to sacrifice freedom for safety – in a similar way to that portrayed in the film *V for Vendetta*.

The late Professor Stephen Hawking warned in 2017 that humans face being superseded by computers if the race to develop artificial intelligence continues apace. Speaking at the Global Mobile Internet Conference in Beijing he said:

I believe that the rise of powerful AI will either be the best thing, or the worst thing, to happen to humanity. I have to say now that we do not yet know which. But we should do all we can to ensure that its future development benefits us and our environment.

I see the development of AI as a trend with its own problems that we know must be dealt with now and into the future. The progress in AI research and development is swift and perhaps we should all stop for a moment and focus our research, not only on making AI more capable but on maximizing its societal benefit.

We're at the most dangerous moment in the history of humanity.

Hawking believed technology has advanced to the point where there is no real difference between what can be achieved by a human brain and a computer.

Computers can in theory emulate human intelligence and exceed it. So we cannot know if we will be infinitely helped by AI or ignored by it and sidelined or conceivably destroyed by it.

Indeed we have concerns that clever machines will be capable of undertaking work currently done by humans and swiftly destroy millions of jobs.

Hawking said he feared technological creation could one day become uncontrollable, resulting in humans being overthrown by systems that were built to serve.

I fear the consequences of creating something that can match or surpass humans. AI would take off on its own and redesign itself at an ever-increasing rate. Humans, who are limited by slow biological evolution, couldn't compete and would be superseded.

Artificial intelligence has long been the subject of science fiction writing – perhaps most influentially with the work of Isaac Asimov and his development of the three laws of robotics, which first appeared in his 1942 short story "Runaround":

1. A robot may not injure a human being or, through inaction, allow a human being to come to harm.
2. A robot must obey the orders given it by human beings except where such orders would conflict with the First Law.
3. A robot must protect its own existence as long as such protection does not conflict with the First or Second Laws.

He added a fourth, zeroth, law when he wrote about the future time when robots would take responsibility for human government:

> 4. A robot may not harm humanity, or, by inaction, allow humanity to come to harm.

These laws have been modified over time but they are increasingly the subject of academic debate. As artificial intelligence develops, the prospect of robots becoming conscious (and we are far from clear what this means) becomes closer. Already robots can learn by themselves and the prospect of them being able to self-replicate by producing other robots lies in the not too far distant future.

Alan Turing, the famous British mathematician, produced the so-called 'Turing test' to determine whether or not a robot can convince a judge that it is actually human. A human is placed in front of a computer terminal in one room and this is connected to a computer terminal in another room. The human can ask any questions it wants and if the replies do not enable the human to be able to tell whether or not these replies are generated by a human or artificial intelligence, then there is no distinction between the two.

Professor Mark Riedl, from the Georgia Institute of Technology, proposed a new test. It would ask a machine to create a convincing poem, story or painting. The test is called Lovelace 2.0 and is a development of a previous Lovelace Test, proposed in 2001. The original test required an AI to create something that it would be incapable of explaining how it was created. Professor Riedl said:

> For the test, the artificial agent passes if it develops a creative artefact from a subset of artistic genres deemed to require human-level intelligence and the artefact meets certain creative constraints given by a human evaluator.

Creativity is not unique to human intelligence, but it is one of the hallmarks of human intelligence.

The artefact could be music, poetry, painting, sculpture or anything else that a human being could regard as art. Exhibitions have already been held of art produced by AI, and AI is already being used to produce new and innovative music.

There are some who think that human beings have creative abilities that AI does not. For instance Professor Alan Woodward, from the University of Surrey, thinks it could help make a key distinction.

I think this new test shows that we all now recognise that humans are more than just very advanced machines, and that creativity is one of those features that separates us from computers – for now.

However, David Wood, chairman of the London Futurists, is not convinced.

It's a popular view that humans differ fundamentally from AIs because humans possess creativity whereas AIs only follow paths of strict rationality.

This is a comforting view, but I think it's wrong. There are already robots that manifest rudimentary emotional intelligence and computers can already write inspiring music.

The trend seems to be clear – AI will be able to duplicate and even surpass all human behaviour. In August 2017, a major orchestra was conducted by a robot who had been trained for the task and was generally considered to have accomplished the task with reasonable effectiveness – this potential will only increase.

The abilities of artificial intelligence are already quite extraordinary. Their computational power is prodigious and as Google and Microsoft's programmes have demonstrated they can interact with human beings and provide information and services that would be beyond the capacity of the most efficient of secretaries. With their ability to access a vast array of data from across cyberspace and to have intimate knowledge of human beings' shopping habits, interests, hobbies, sexual preferences and social life, they can know individual human beings intimately (at least when this is defined in terms of their shopping preferences and behaviour). Increasingly human introductions and dating are done online, and films such as *Her* show the increasing possibility of romantic relationships between human beings and AI. The increasing sophistication of Japanese sex robots when combined with the latest developments in AI raise the possibility of marriage between human beings and AI. To many people, these developments seem farfetched but there are already men in Japan who would prefer a relationship with such an entity rather than a human being. In the Netherlands, prostitution services are available with AI at a considerably lower cost than with a human being.

Within twenty years, the world will face an economic problem of unprecedented size as more and more jobs will be taken over by AI taxis, bus and lorry drivers will be replaced, teacher numbers will be significantly reduced, much of the work of solicitors and judges will be handed over to AI, there is already AI which can design and even build houses – there are very few jobs that AI will not be able to do as effectively and as well as human beings. Some commentators have claimed that the effect of AI on the labour market has been overdone as new jobs will arise. Similar concerns were raised when tractors replaced horses yet new jobs driving tractors and maintaining them quickly arose. The situation is, however, different with AI as it is vastly cheaper and more reliable than human labour, and as finance is always the major factor, the incentive for companies to reduce costs by using AI instead of humans is very great – not least because AI does not need rest breaks, can work without sleeping and is more reliable. AI also does not pay tax and this will have a considerable effect on government revenues. The attractiveness of a minimum wage for human workers is very real and an important and necessary development, but it must be recognised that higher minimum wages will simply accentuate the move to replace human workers with AI.

President Donald Trump's original choice for Labor Secretary Andrew Puzder, the head of several big fast food companies, is happy with fewer labourers. He's an advocate of automated customer services:

> They're always polite, they always upsell, they never take a vacation, they never show up late, there's never a slip-and-fall, or an age, sex, or race-discrimination case.
> (BBC, *The World This Weekend*, 26th December 2016)

One respected economist argues this will get a lot worse. Professor Richard Baldwin predicts, among other things, that:

> Hotel rooms in London could be cleaned by people driving robots sitting in Kenya or Buenos Aires or wherever, for a tenth of the cost here.

He has a simple view of people's political reaction – "Boy, are they going to be angry!" He is, in fact, behind the times as there will be no need for someone to 'drive' a cleaning robot – as the Japanese have shown they can be fully autonomous and carry out their tasks with no human intervention.

This is going to have major effects on the social order as many people will not have jobs. Even if everyone is provided with a basic wage whether or not they work (this has been suggested in some European countries although how this can be afforded is debatable) the sense of meaning that comes from productive work will have been eroded. What is more, tax revenues will decline as AI and robots do not pay tax and this will have a major effect on government revenues.

The British Standards Institute has issued a more official version of Asimov's robotic laws aimed at helping designers create ethically sound robots. The document, BS8611 Robots and robotic devices, is aimed at establishing ethical standards for robots or AI. Welcoming the guidelines at the Social Robotics and AI conference in Oxford, Alan Winfield, a professor of robotics at the University of the West of England, said they represented, "the first step towards embedding ethical values into robotics and AI". "As far as I know this is the first published standard for the ethical design of robots."

Winfield said after the event, "It's a bit more sophisticated than Asimov's laws – it basically sets out how to do an ethical risk assessment of a robot."

The BSI document begins with some broad ethical principles:

Robots should not be designed solely or primarily to kill or harm humans; humans, not robots, are the responsible agents; it should be possible to find out who is responsible for any robot and its behaviour.

It goes on to highlight a range of more contentious issues, such as whether an emotional bond with a robot is desirable, particularly when the robot is designed to interact with children or the elderly.

Noel Sharkey, emeritus professor of robotics and AI at the University of Sheffield, said this was an example of where robots could unintentionally deceive us. "There was a recent study where little robots were embedded in a nursery school," he said:

The children loved them and actually bonded with the robots. But when asked afterwards, the children clearly thought the robots were more cognitive than their family pet.

In fact the British standard is unrealistic as most major countries are developing AI systems which can be used to provide lethal force. In the military area drones are increasingly being used not just in the air but also on the ground and underwater. Boeing's new AI-driven submarine has been described as 'awesome', it is completely autonomous and can stay at sea for six months at a time without needing to refuel. China has a hypersonic, fully automated fighter aircraft in development. Increasingly AI is being introduced into military hardware and several governments are developing, or have already developed, autonomous military capabilities which are able to take lethal action without human intervention. This can speed up response times which is a key factor in military strategic planning.

Increasingly the boundaries between humans and AI are becoming blurred. Elon Musk, the head of Tesla and SpaceX, is investing hundreds of millions of dollars in developing the latest forms of AI. In September 2017, Russian President Vladimir Putin said, "Artificial intelligence is the future, not only of Russia, but of all of mankind," and "Whoever becomes the leader in this sphere will become the ruler of the world." After seeing Putin's comments Elon Musk tweeted that: "competition for AI superiority at national level (is the) most likely cause of WW3."

Musk's companies and Google are in a race to develop the most advanced forms of AI (although Russia is probably in the lead in weaponizing AI). Musk is working on integrating cyberspace with the human brain. With an ambitious goal of keeping mankind up-to-speed with advancing technology, the *Wall Street Journal* in August 2017 announced that Elon Musk has played an active role in launching a new company called Neuralink which seeks to create devices that can be implanted in the human brain. However, such a step inevitably raises questions of who will be in control of the digital space that would emerge.

Already smart phones are ubiquitous and human beings rely on them for information and social interaction. If, instead of having a smart phone, access to cyberspace could be integrated into the human brain this would provide immediate access to all that the web can offer and could radically increase human capabilities. The plan to directly link the brain with AI will inevitably create a privileged class that will be able to dominate the rest of humanity – most of whom will not have jobs. Even in today's world, the jobs that do exist are increasingly at minimum pay levels and whilst unemployment in the West is generally at low rates, most of those jobs are already at such low pay levels that families find it increasingly difficult to make ends meet and have to rely on increasing volumes of debt.

Some readers may consider this scenario as unduly apocalyptic, but the evidence is all around us already. Supermarket checkout assistants and station forecourt operators are increasingly being replaced by machines. In Japan, robot nurses are looking after old people, and Japan already has five hotels run entirely by AI staff with no human beings in attendance at all. Factories across the world, particularly in China and the US, are replacing factory line workers with AI to reduce costs. Musk has warned that AI provides the greatest existential threat to human beings at the same time as he is one of the leaders in developing advanced AI. In September 2017 he predicted the next major war would be between military AI and has urged regulation – but there is no sign of this being actively considered. Nevertheless, Musk clearly has a vision to place AI at the centre of transportation of all types, manufacturing, human interaction of all forms and, of course, the cyber world.

Slovakian philosopher Professor Slavoj Žižek is a leading figure challenging Elon Musk's vision:

Here I don't believe in those dreamers like [American scientist] Ray Kurzweil, who think we will become part of some collective brain-singularity and so on. No, the only question for me is – and we don't have a good answer – how will this affect our self-experience? Will we still experience ourselves as free beings, or will we be regulated by digital machinery – now comes the crucial point – without even being aware that we are being regulated?

Žižek argues that with advancing technology, it will be possible to use this AI link to control people and get them to do things without even realising it, something that has totalitarian implications.

Never forget that attempts to control us always begin like this [Žižek explained]. You begin with all these humanitarian causes, heart diseases and so on, and then sooner or later you move to police control. Even today, computers know more about ourselves than we do.

I know where the future is. We will be automatically checked-up, controlled for our health, but also for our purchases, what are we buying, for our political opinions, for our voting, and so on. A computer will literally know us better than we know ourselves.

I'm not opposed to this, I'm not a utopian, my question is simply: who will control the computers?

Žižek, who has written extensively about the class struggle, said he predicts a new class system emerging, built around our access to the digital world.

I think we are approaching a paradoxical situation [in light of modern consumerism], where to be outside digital space will become a privilege. I think the privileged will be those who will be able to regulate digital space without themselves being fully included into it.

A new class division will appear, much stronger than the old class division envisioned by Marxist theory: a division between those who are just controlled, and those who can regulate those modes of digital control themselves.

I'm not a pessimist here. It's just we should be aware that something radically new is emerging which will affect our most basic experience of who we are as human beings.

Critics of AI such as Stephen Hawking receive some publicity but real efforts to control the development of advanced AI and humans may prove impossible. There is no world government and every company in different countries round the world seeks to reduce costs and campaigns for a minimum of regulation. Even if, say, the European Union succeeded in putting in place laws regulating development, other countries such as China and South Korea would not be affected.

If the advent of AI is combined with genetic engineering (p. 115) and the integration of the cyber world with human brains, then the possibility of a new, enhanced race of human beings may emerge. For some the prospects of this are exciting but it raises real questions about what it means to be human and whether something important, or indeed essential, may be lost in the process. Some have suggested that we are perhaps thirty years away from the Singularity – this is not the singularity that gave rise to the universe in the initial 'Big Bang' which occurred about 13.7 billion years ago. The new Singularity would evolve with the rapid development of AI which would foster the development of new and more comprehensive super intelligence until there eventually emerged a global intelligence system which controlled everything on the planet. If human beings were effectively part of this global intelligence network then they, too, would form part of a single consciousness. At the 2012 Singularity Summit, Professor Stuart Armstrong undertook a study of artificial intelligence predictions by experts and, although he found a wide range of predicted dates, they nevertheless had a median date of 2040 for the Singularity to occur.

At present these ideas lie in the realm of science fiction or perhaps scientific conjecture, but they represent hypotheses that are taken seriously by many scientists and entrepreneurs. If anything like these ideas come to fruition, they would involve the eventual extinction or subservience of human beings as the new self-conscious AI would simply render them redundant.

Peter Singer, as outlined in Chapter 4, would specifically sanction and approve the killing of full-term disabled babies on the grounds that their quality of life would be poor. Better, he argues, to kill the disabled baby and to have another one whose quality of life would be better. This position makes complete intellectual sense provided that human beings are simply advanced animals and the idea of a transcendent or Eternal dimension to human life is rejected. In spite, however, of its rational plausibility, these ideas are anathema to many – but Peter Singer regards such a reaction as primitive and to be dismissed. If there is no Eternal dimension to human lives, nothing that separates us from advanced animals or, in principle, AI, then transhumanism and a quality of life ethic make complete sense. It may well be, however, that these represent an impoverishment of what it means to be human.

These questions bring together the different themes underlying this book – namely the issue of truth, what it means to be human and whether the idea of an Eternal dimension has any relevance in the modern world. Instead of congratulating ourselves on creating AI that may be able to replicate much if not all of the behaviour of the average human being or instead of relishing our ability to eliminate disease and to enable some, wealthy human beings to be genetically perfect (however that might be defined), we should be focussing on reminding the average human being of their potential to become 'fully human' – fully what they are capable of being at their best. The focus should be on helping people to come back to a realisation of the potential and capacities of human beings and to encourage them on a path to fulfil this potential. This has been the essential message of all religion down the ages although it has been blunted by dogma and ritual. The alternative is to see human beings as no more than functional biological robots designed to carry out certain tasks and to feel 'happy' whilst doing so – even if this means genetically altering future generations so that depression and despair is eliminated and people become content with their lot. The result is not an enhancement of humanity but a diminution.

The alternatives can be expressed clearly and remarkably simply. Which would we prefer:

1) To have a capacity for human freedom, altruism, the appreciation of beauty and genuine love and commitment even if these are combined with the ability to sometimes suffer, to be betrayed by friends and lovers, and to experience failure and to sometimes have our dreams turn to dust. All these are part of a traditional view of what it means to be human grounded in the common human nature we all share. The Greeks recognised this and so does the Natural Law tradition of ethics which has been a central part of a Western understanding of humanity for two thousand years. This approach emphasises our common human potential and calls people to seek to fulfil this potential by standing up for Eternal values even if this may cause short-term pain and distress.

2) Not to suffer, to be economically effective and successful, to be relatively disease free and to be happy even if this

means that human freedom and human potentiality are significantly constrained.

In the film *The Matrix*, the character Cypher betrayed his friends in order to achieve the second of these alternatives because living in the truth was simply too painful and too difficult. He just wanted to be happy and to forget reality or what his situation really was (namely part of a programmed neural network where almost everything that he experienced was an illusion). Many today would make the same choice and opt for the second alternative. If the aim in life is simply to be happy, then it seems a perfectly reasonable option. If, however, human potential is destined for something more than this, then to opt for the second choice is to deliberately choose not to fulfil human potential and to turn our backs on the path to becoming fully human. It is to debase ourselves.

Part Two

Re-Kindling The Flame

Chapter Six

In Defence of Truth and the Relevance of Education

The materialist, verificationist and atheist views of the world are convincing and intellectually plausible. Natural selection can, indeed, explain a great deal and humans clearly share a great deal of animal genetics and animal behaviour. Since the dawn of recorded history, however, humans have always felt that there was more to life than can be accounted for by sense perception. They believed in a transcendent, Eternal reality, and tried to give expression to this through various religious approaches. Today some of the most intelligent, well balanced, widely read and 'good' (in a non-trivial sense) people in history still want to make a similar affirmation. They maintain that absolute Truth exists and is worth striving for, and that this Truth cannot be arrived at by purely empirical means. I have devoted my life to philosophy but some of the most wonderful (both intellectually and humanly) people I have known have shared this belief. Reason alone will not reveal it and many highly intelligent people are perfectly capable of denying its existence.

A search for the Eternal opens up the possibility of a broader vision of reality and of accountability to a fundamental order of the universe. It is the wellspring of creativity and the arts as well as a search for the common good. Nowhere is this more clearly expressed than by William Blake who has influenced, among countless others, the British novelist Philip Pullman. Pullman is sometimes denigrated by some religious believers as an atheist, but he has a profound commitment to a spiritual dimension to reality and identifies with Blake's view of a 'fourfold' vision:

1. Fourfold vision stands for supreme delight which is found

in a state of ecstatic or mystical bliss – this is the final end of religious mystics.

2. Threefold arises naturally from poetry and dreams where contraries can be equally true and which call us beyond the routine of the normal world.

3. Twofold vision denotes seeing not only with the eye but through it, seeing context and connections, associations and emotional meanings.

4. Single vision – this is the literal, rational, unreflective view of the world. It is this approach that the verificationists and the materialists adopt, and yet they seem incapable of seeing beyond what science and a verificationist approach to reality can convey.

Pullman considers single vision to be deadly – and he is right. Creativity is a central part of human potentiality.

A story might illustrate the basic point. For many years I was vice-principal of the University of London College which specialised in theology and philosophy. It had the largest theological library in Britain (the only possible rival being the Bodleian in Oxford). My predecessor as vice-principal was a Jesuit (a member of the Catholic religious order, the Society of Jesus). He was a brilliant philosopher with the ability to spot a dodgy argument with incredible rapidity and with great precision. He was a gentle man yet as a philosopher he had few rivals in his field. I knew him well and respected him greatly. During one of many interviews I recorded with him he told me the following story (and this, it must be emphasised, was a man of total integrity to whom I would have willingly entrusted my life if I had needed to). He was studying for his Master's degree in philosophy at Oxford University as a young Jesuit prior to training to become a Catholic priest. As might be expected he took to his studies like a duck to water and thoroughly enjoyed them. He used to spend an hour each morning in prayer in the chapel before starting his studies and one day, quite suddenly, he realised that he did not believe in God – he did not believe at all. To him this was devastating. He had set out to dedicate his life to God but his studies had convinced him that God did not exist. What he found most extraordinary was that he felt that he could not stop going to the chapel to pray as he felt as if he was "betraying a friend". Intellectually he realised this was nonsense – how can one betray something that does not exist? He had, of course, read the writings of Freud and many others on psychology and told himself that this reaction must simply have been the result of social conditioning from his childhood, but he nevertheless could not prevent himself. The psychological, reductionist explanation of what he was experiencing just did not fit with his experience.

About a month later, the Jesuit Provincial (the head of the Society of Jesus in Britain) came round to see him – the Provincial was required to see every member of the Society each year. The Provincial breezed into the meeting (his words relayed to me) and said what good reports he had had about the young man's studies. However, the young man told him, with some hesitation, that he was going to be forced to leave the Society since he no longer believed in God. This, surprisingly, did not seem to shock the Provincial. The young man asked if he could continue his studies, staying in the Jesuit house in Oxford and leave when his studies were over, and the Provincial readily agreed. The Provincial suggested he should talk with a former spiritual director of the young man which he did – also explaining to this director that he could not stop going to the chapel and that he no longer believed in God. This director asked him whether he had changed his mind since starting his studies at Oxford and he answered that, of course, this was the case since this is the whole point of philosophy – to seek Truth.

To cut a long story short, he stayed in the Society, still convinced that God did not exist and still unable to stop going into the chapel to pray. At length, and it took several years, he recognised he either had to trust his head or his heart and he made the decision to stay in the Society, to become a priest and, sixty years later, has never regretted his decision. His intellect wrestled with the difficulty of belief in God but he came to realise that the intellect alone is not sufficient. The reductionist explanations of the philosophers simply did not fit with his experience.

Now it would be easy to reject this story and for the reader to say that he must have been conditioned by his upbringing, to say that he must have feared losing meaning if he left the Society, that he was not intelligent enough to be able to see the nonsense of his position. These would be reasonable points for someone who did not know him. I knew him very well – he was and is a man of the utmost integrity, a man of quite brilliant ability and someone who would always pursue Truth at whatever cost. Countless thousands of other similar stories could be relayed, many of them by prominent scientists, mathematicians and philosophers. Blaise Pascal, the great mathematician, said:

The heart has its reasons which reason knows nothing of.

It is readily possible to dismiss such experiences if one is a verificationist or a materialist. Nevertheless the Oxford Religious Experience Research unit has collected tens of thousands of reports of religious experiences from around the world. To dismiss such reports on the basis of a preconceived set of assumptions, which are increasingly recognised as flawed, is not the mark of high intelligence or an openminded search for Truth. Abductive arguments (p. 118) demand that consideration should be given to a much broader array of factors. To dismiss such widespread and persuasive factors on the basis of a priori, materialist assumption is now widely recognised as inadequate.

The Danish philosopher Søren Kierkegaard (1813–1855),

whom Ludwig Wittgenstein described as the greatest philosopher of the 19th century and a saint, reacted against the dominant Hegelian philosophy of his day. Hegel was the first to produce a philosophy of history and he argued that truth emerges as a result of a dialectical process. An idea, a thesis, is put forward and this provokes an alternative view – an antithesis. Differences between the two positions seem contradictory but, over time, they come to be reconciled and a new consensus, a new thesis emerges. This provokes an inevitable reaction and gives rise to an antithesis. The two positions seem irreconcilable but, over time, a new consensus, a new thesis emerges. This gives rise to another new antithesis and, again, the two positions seem irreconcilable but, over time, a new consensus, a new thesis emerges. So the process continues over time. The nickname given to Hegel's position was 'both/and' to reflect the fact that both thesis and antithesis claim truth. Against this, Kierkegaard protested and the nickname given to his position was 'either/or'. There are absolute truths at stake and they are either true or they are false. It may not be possible in some cases to prove which are true and which are false, but Kierkegaard argued that lack of proof is not the same as lack of truth. Intuitively any child and most adults will accept his position today.

'Truth decay', or a shift away from interest in seeking Truth or any reliance on evidence, may be a defining characteristic of our current age. Thus wrote Michael Rich and Jennifer Kavanagh in a book which featured on President Obama's 2018 reading list (*Truth Decay: An Initial Exploration of the Diminishing Role of Facts and Analysis in American Public Life*, 2018). The whole of modern culture, as we have seen, seems to reinforce the idea that we live in a post-truth world. However, the idea that truth is dead is nonsense. Many people nod sagely given the widespread acceptance of the claim that absolute Truth is an idea whose time has passed but it really does not stand up to a moment's analysis. In every sphere of life, truth matters and is an absolute.

- Either there are green worms on the moon or there are not.
- Either the earth is flat or it is not.
- Either water can turn to ice or it cannot.
- Either Hitler knew about the concentration camps and the mass extermination of Jews, Gypsies, homosexuals and others or he did not.
- Either Muhammad had the Qur'an revealed to him by the Archangel or he did not.
- Either humans will survive death or they will not.
- Either there are absolute values in the universe or there are not.
- Either smoking increases the risk of lung cancer or it does not.
- Either the Loch Ness Monster exists or it does not.

Any child of five will accept that absolute truth exists. It is good to be reminded of Hans Christian Andersen's fairy tale of *The Emperor's New Clothes*. Some weavers convinced the Emperor that they could make magnificent, magical clothes which could only be seen by those who were wise. When they put the invisible clothes on the Emperor, he and the rest of his court did not want to say that he was naked as then they would show themselves not to be wise. It took a young boy to shout out, "He's naked!" before everyone else had the courage to say the same. It is similar with the claim that we live in a post-truth world.

Of course, in some cases there is ambiguity and different perspectives. In a rape trial, there can be different perspectives on what is regarded as consent and what is not; in history there can be many different viewpoints on events; in economics there can be multiple explanations for a financial crisis; in a marriage breakdown there are always complex reasons which are generally not fully understood; in any human action there are multifaceted conscious and unconscious motivations; there are multiple moral and political frameworks and little agreement about aesthetics.

No one doubts that truth is complex and may be difficult if not hard to determine. No one doubts that simplistic accounts of what is 'true' and 'false' are inadequate and misleading. None of these, however, mean that Truth does not exist – simply that it is necessary to be humble and to recognise that any claim to absolute Truth must be treated with caution and real life is far more complex than may appear to be the case.

Nowhere is contemporary relativism, nihilism and a post-truth culture challenged more effectively than by mathematics. Plato argued that mathematics underpinned the whole of reality as well as, for instance, beauty, harmony in music and the very idea of 'The Good'. Over the entrance of his School of Philosophy in Athens were the words, "Let no one unskilled in mathematics enter here". Mathematicians have long been aware of the central question underpinning their discipline: "Is mathematics something that is discovered or is it created by human beings?"

If mathematics exists and human beings discover the law of mathematics, then not everything is relative. There are some absolute truths – at the very least these would be the fundamental laws of mathematics. From these, many other truths can be derived. Mathematics underpins a great deal of the natural world including the number of rabbits that are bred under ideal conditions, the spirals on a sunflower or on every fir cone that exists, the structure of the human body (Leonardo da Vinci's *Vitruvian Man*, the first image to ever leave the solar system, has every bone in the body constructed on a mathematical basis). Mathematics underpins the way the whole of reality behaves.

Leonardo Pisano is better known by his nickname of Fibonacci and lived around 1170–1250 CE. The sequence that Fibonacci discovered (the Fibonacci sequence) seems to underlie a great deal of the natural world. There is a real sense in which the natural world forms patterns that are mathematical. Surgeons use this sequence and the 'Golden Number' which derives from it when performing some forms of cosmetic surgery as if proportions are right, then beauty emerges. Great artists have used the mathematics of proportion in constructing parts of their paintings. Numbers are everywhere and seem to be an absolute which mathematicians discover. Frequently, when a new formula is covered, a mathematician will describe it as beautiful because it is simple and elegant.

Professor Max Tegmark, in his book *Our Mathematical Universe: My Quest for the Ultimate Nature of Reality* (Random House/Knopf, 2014), said:

What's the answer to the ultimate question of life, the universe, and everything? In Douglas Adams' science-fiction spoof *The Hitchhiker's Guide to the Galaxy*, the answer was found to be 42; the hardest part turned out to be finding the real question. I find it very appropriate that Douglas Adams joked about 42, because mathematics has played a striking role in our growing understanding of our Universe.

The Higgs Boson was predicted with the same tool as the discovery of the planet Neptune and the radio wave: with mathematics. Galileo famously stated that our Universe is a "grand book" written in the language of mathematics. Because of our education system, many people equate mathematics with arithmetic. Yet mathematicians study abstract structures far more diverse than numbers, including geometric shapes. If one throws a pebble, the beautiful shape that nature makes for its trajectory is based on mathematics! The trajectories of anything you throw have the same shape, called an upside-down parabola. When we observe how things move around in orbits in space, we discover another recurring shape: the ellipse. Moreover, these two shapes are related: the tip of a very elongated ellipse is shaped almost exactly like a parabola, so in fact, all of these trajectories are simply parts of ellipses.

There's something very mathematical about our Universe, and that the more carefully we look, the more math we seem to find... if we assume that reality exists independently of humans, then for a description to be complete, it must also be well-defined according to non-human entities – aliens or supercomputers, say – that lack any understanding of human concepts. That brings us to the Mathematical Universe Hypothesis, which states that our external physical reality is a mathematical structure.

Bertrand Russell, one of the great atheist philosophers of the 20th century, was firmly convinced of the reality of mathematics. He said:

> I have wished to understand the hearts of men.
> I have wished to know why the stars shine.
> And I have tried to apprehend the Pythagorean power
> by which number holds sway above the flux.
> (Prologue to Russell's *Autobiography*)

The first line refers to psychology, the second to physics but the third reference to the "Pythagorean Power" relates to mathematics which underpins the whole of the changing universe (the flux). According to Plato, Bertrand Russell, Mandelbrot, Roger Penrose and almost every mathematician, mathematical reality does exist independent of human observations. Mathematics is about discovering reality. Professor Roger Penrose is one of the greatest mathematicians of the contemporary era. In his 1989 book *The Emperor's New Mind: Concerning Computers, Minds and The Laws of Physics* (Oxford University Press), he looked at the internal structure of math. After reviewing the Cauchy Integral Formula, the Riemann Mapping Theorem and the Lewy Extension property, Penrose argued that the beauty and structure of mathematics is there waiting to be discovered. Mathematicians can communicate because they share a common, universal, frame of reference. (Lindström, 2000, "Quasi-Realism in mathematics". *Monist*, 83, 122–149) Penrose found that almost every major mathematician (there are a few exceptions such as Gödel) is a closet Platonist and when they explore mathematics they see themselves as uncovering the fundamental ground rules of the universe.

The potentiality of the universe that was inbuilt within the singularity is essentially mathematical. The more we understand of the quantum world, the more we realise that the language of mathematics is the only way we can begin to approximate to its reality. If, as seems almost unquestionably to be the case, the laws of mathematics are something that humans discover and not something that they create, then not all truth is relative. There are absolutes in the universe and Truth does exist.

What, then, does 'post-truth' mean if it does not mean that Truth is dead? As might be expected, there are multiple meanings:

1) In a world dominated by sound bites and by the media with brief headlines in newspapers and even briefer accounts of events on smart phones; in a world dominated by powerful media interests each with their own agenda it becomes exceptionally hard to access what is really true, what is partially true and what is entirely false. We come to accept as true those stories that we find congenial and which fit into our world-view. We are lazy. We do not want to look beneath the surface and to question and challenge. Our lives are so busy and the constant sources of information which we select to watch (generally based on our own preconceptions of which media source is most reliable – which essentially means which fits in with our own view of the world) – are so limited, that we have

little time or inclination to look beneath the surface. We therefore accept superficial understandings of what is true and make our judgements based on these. It is not that we live in a post-truth world but that we are willing to accept superficial accounts of truth. It is not Truth that has died but rather our interest in looking for it.

2) Democracy is a disaster. Plato rejected it as a form of government and Churchill said that it was the worst form of governments apart from all the alternatives. The problems are all too clear – democracy means pandering to the interests of the least educated in society (as they are the most numerous and therefore most influential in voting terms). The problem with this is not so much lack of education but the ease with which large numbers of poorly educated people who have little incentive, wish or ability to think deeply about complex questions can be easily influenced by the popular media controlled by those with power and influence. This means that long-term thinking in the best interests of a country and its people is ignored in favour of what is popular on a short-term basis, since this is what will achieve electoral success for those who seek power. Access to the media is essential for ideas to be disseminated and only those with media access can have their voices heard. Those who dissent, those who argue for complexity of narratives or who reject the dominant paradigm are silenced by being given no voice. Demagogues triumph. Those who control the media are well aware of this and they have the real power today – not the politicians who can all too easily be manipulated by their need for favourable media exposure. As Justice Louis D. Brandeis (1856–1941) said speaking of the United States:

We can have democracy in this country, or we can have great wealth concentrated in the hands of a few, but we can't have both.
(Quoted by Ralph Nader in his Presidential campaign in 2000)

Or former President Jimmy Carter:

We've become, now, an oligarchy instead of a democracy. I think that's been the worst damage to the basic moral and ethical standards to the American political system that I've ever seen in my life.
(In an interview with Oprah Winfrey on *Super Soul Sunday*)

It is the power of the media controlled by the wealthy few that has, more than any other single factor, given rise to the supposedly post-truth world in which we live. As Milton said:

And what are the people but a herd confused,
A miscellaneous rabble who extol
Things vulgar, and well weighed, scarce worth the praise?
They praise, and they admire they know not what,
And know not whom, but as one leads the other.
(Milton, *Paradise Regained*, Book 3)

3) Young people are brought up by their parents to view the world, history, politics and reality itself through the same spectacles that they wear (which is why Socrates, as we have seen, was put to death by the middle-class citizens of Athens [399 BCE]). Education reinforces this process and politicians choose education systems and, in many cases, educational content in schools to serve what they see as the essential priorities – and these have little to do with Truth. They are primarily concerned with creating

economically effective units to produce wealth which will enable a consumerist society to have all the things it wants whether these be consumer goods, food, infrastructure, sex, health, pensions, entertainment and old age care or defence. The interests that are being fostered are, in reality, not those of all members of society but of a narrow elite which controls the media and politics for their own interests. These interests include having a docile workforce kept entertained by shopping and trivia. Nowhere is this more the case than in the United States where hundreds of millions of dollars are needed to run for President and these funds are provided by interest groups who want their own priorities to be promoted. The NRA (the National Rifle Association which campaigns for unregulated access to guns of every type) is a good example. The same applies, perhaps to a lesser extent, in almost all democracies. Small groups like the Carlton Club in St James in London (whose membership consists largely of immensely wealthy and influential Conservative politicians) control or represent the interests of the most powerful and wealthy in society and use these interests to foster the power and privilege of the elite. Above all they seek to ensure that 'they' are kept in power and that the influence of 'the others' (those poorly educated, outside their own social circle or with alternative visions of economics or politics) are kept silent. This is not done by the activities of a police state as in totalitarian regimes but by ownership and control of the media, sporting outlets and the like.

Serious questions about the aims and purposes of education are deliberately marginalised. Fifty years ago in Western universities there were philosophy of education departments which were concerned with fundamental questions about the nature and purpose of education – almost all of these have now been closed and it is left to politicians to decide (with their very clear, if unstated, vested interests) what the purposes and aims of education are.

4) Because of the increasing complexity of the modern world, knowledge has become severely compartmentalized. In the early part of the 19th century it was, broadly, possible to be widely read and to have a reasonably detailed knowledge of most aspects of science, politics, religion and economics. This is no longer the case. Specialisation starts in the last two years of school (and often earlier), it narrows once a degree choice is made and the process of limiting the focus continues thereafter. People become more and more knowledgeable about an increasingly restricted range of material and, even then, find it is difficult to look beneath the surface level paradigms into which they have been educated. Academic specialization at universities contributes to this with the need to submit papers to refereed journals (read by few other academics) and to chase 'citations'. This gives rise to the iniquitous business of academics citing each other in order to ensure funding for themselves and their university departments. Anyone seeking to challenge the orthodoxy in their own field is unlikely to be published and will find their funding dries up as they may well lose their academic post. Finance, citations and promotions in the academic world are now closely linked. Few specialists have the time or the funding to be able to disseminate their knowledge except to fellow academics, and securing funding for research becomes paramount for all scientists. This means that the direction of research is driven by those who provide the funding and this accentuates bias and partiality. Ordinary people lose confidence in 'experts' and this leads to the rise of dominance of the orator. Socrates warned of the danger of

oratory – speaking well and wisdom are often not linked. Franklin Roosevelt said:

Democracy cannot succeed unless those who express their choice are prepared to choose wisely. The real safeguard of democracy, therefore, is education.

Or as Isaac Asimov said:

There is a cult of ignorance in the United States, and there has always been. The strain of anti-intellectualism has been a constant thread winding its way through our political and cultural life, nurtured by the false notion that democracy means that my ignorance is just as good as your knowledge.

("A Cult of Ignorance", Asimov, 1980)

The election of President Trump was a powerful example of this as was the British conservative politician Michael Gove with his dismissal of expert opinion as of no more value than uninformed opinion so that, instead of listening to knowledgeable experts, people could be controlled by those who dominate the media. It is not a coincidence that the first interview with the newly-elected President Trump was by Michael Gove and it was only later disclosed that Rupert Murdoch was an unseen presence in the room at the same time.

Democracy is an ideal form of government – provided those voting are properly informed, thoughtful and able to dispassionately analyse alternative positions, yet we are further and further away from this ideal. The solution is not to abandon democracy but to improve education of those who have the responsibility of voting so that, the majority of them at least, can be better informed and not accept the glib certainties that they are fed and which they so willingly repeat. 'Education' here does not mean an increasing focus on STEM (Science, Technology, Engineering and Mathematics) subjects but a broad curriculum which has as its aim a pre-vocation education helping young people to think deeply and well about fundamental questions, and what it means to be human and to fulfil human potential.

The need is not to accept a post-truth world but to challenge it – and this is a task that schools need to take particularly seriously. They are, however, prevented from doing so by a (deliberate?) narrowing of education. If people do not seek Truth, they are much easier to manipulate. If they do not believe Truth exists, they will not be concerned about it. Instead of a broad vision of education the focus has been switched to concentration on constant testing through a child's schooling culminating in a results-based focus in the final years. These tests, in themselves, become self-fulfilling prophesies as teachers are aware of the most recent rounds of tests and adjust their expectations of children accordingly so that the chances of 'late developers' being recognised are much reduced. What counts as mattering throughout the educational process are the grades that a child achieves. Parents judge schools on the basis of grade performance, government inspectors use grade performance as a litmus test when judging schools, governing bodies of schools demand improvements in grades from the head teachers. Heads and senior management of schools reinforce the centrality of achievement which can be measured in terms of examination success and teachers are judged accordingly. In some independent schools, efforts are made to recruit the brightest students in order to improve positions in league tables and, at the other end of the academic spectrum, to sometimes encourage (sometimes force) those who are less gifted academically to leave so that the academic results of the school will not be adversely affected. The result is that students are spoon-fed 'gobbits' or essential information needed to answer questions in examinations. They no longer read books – this takes too much time. Instead they are provided with summaries which prevent them engaging in complexity and seeing or even seeking alternative views. Their reading is often confined to short 'tweets' on their mobile devices or the ephemera of those currently in the news. Young people are put under more and more pressure to 'achieve' and this means achievement in terms of grades. They are told that their whole future depends on their grades as these will give access to the best universities, and those who fail to secure the necessary grades are told they will be condemned to life behind a fast food counter (although in the near future there will be few such jobs as AI will have taken most of them).

This vision of education is an impoverishment and fails to prepare young people for the future they will face – this will be a world dominated by Artificial Intelligence where most routine jobs will disappear. Bus, lorry and train drivers, supermarket checkout assistants, hotel receptionists, factory workers, paralegals, accountants, many nurses, teachers, police and armed forces personnel will all become irrelevant once the rise of AI is translated into the world of work. This is, as we have seen, no longer science fiction but is becoming an increasing reality and the speed of replacement of jobs by AI will accelerate rapidly. Instead of a world of work, many young people will face a future where there is little or no work. Within thirty years there will be a crisis of employment with fewer and fewer jobs being available – yet most politicians carefully avoid discussing the catastrophic implications of this. Certainly, there will be some new jobs, but these will be vastly outweighed by the loss of routine jobs which AI can increasingly do more cheaply, efficiently and reliably than their human counterparts. Preparing young people for this new world is not something that politicians, educators, parents and still less students are even considering – but it will not help to marginalise concern for Truth and instead to enforce a cramming system which discourages independent thinking and a passion for open-minded enquiry.

Education requires a commitment to the education of the whole person – almost every school pays lip service to this but few really engage with what it means. Teachers see themselves as responsible for imparting knowledge in their particular subject areas or achieving success in music, the arts or sports – but few ever consider what it means to educate the whole person. There is a spiritual element to this which is often ignored – schools need to nourish the spirit of young people so that they have open, enquiring minds, showing a willingness to challenge conformity and to think independently. Only by so doing can they not only, possibly, seek to fulfil their human potential but also meet the challenges of a new world order. Schools are not programming AI robots to perform tasks – they are (or at least they should be) educating the whole human person. Their task is pre-vocational. Any outstanding head teacher will recognise this and stand up for this vision against pressure from governments, governing bodies and, indeed, parents who all too often have a far narrow vision of what good education means.

Truth does exist – it is simply that most people are no longer interested in seeking it. They have become infected with ennui, with languor, with torpor. Life no longer seems to have any meaning. The only purpose of existence seems to be happy for the short time we are here – and being happy mainly consists of seeking short-term feelings of happiness rather than anything which might endure because, in a world of ephemera, nothing is held to last. People have become like drunken peasants asleep on a cart, intoxicated by a diet of ephemera whilst the horse that pulls the cart takes them they know not where.

John Stuart Mill (1806–1873) the great parliamentarian and utilitarian philosopher recognised this. He was a brilliant young man and his father focused his education on an accumulation of factual knowledge. He had no time for play, for music or friends – the result was an almost complete nervous breakdown when he was 16 years old. Many young people today face similar pressure, and depression and a sense of futility are common. Mill was driven to the poetry of Wordsworth and Coleridge as a remedy for his stunted education and this helped him to develop a much broader approach to utilitarianism. He made a clear distinction between actions which are enjoyable and those which are valuable or worthwhile – enjoyment is measured in terms of short-term feelings whereas what is valuable is what contributes to a human being fulfilling their potential. This distinction is not something that most modern education addresses.

Many things have great value (contribute greatly to a happy life) but can be very unpleasant, like chemotherapy, penicillin shots, punishment and tooth drilling. Many things can be very pleasant, like chocolate, ice cream, tobacco, and hard drugs, but they do not have great value (they do not contribute much to a happy life). For Mill, the value of something is radically different from how it makes us feel yet most education today fails to even try to make this distinction. The value of something requires taking into account:

- the long-term benefits (security, contentment, peace of mind, reputation) and
- the avoidance of long-term pains (for instance cancer, obesity, divorce, loneliness, reputation).

The value of something takes a much broader view than merely consideration of pleasure. Mill was critical of much of the education of his time, and since then the situation has become much worse:

It is, no doubt, a very laudable effort in modern teaching to render as much as possible of what the young are required to learn, easy and interesting to them. But when this principle is pushed to the length of not requiring them to learn anything but what has been made easy and interesting, one of the chief objects of education is sacrificed... (education...) is training up a race of people who will be incapable of doing anything that is disagreeable to them.

(Mill, *Autobiography*, pp. 53 and 55)

The focus on teachers providing summaries and coaching students to get through tests and examinations is a denial of education, it is a denial of a real search for Truth and also a denial of any attempt to ask questions about whether or not life has meaning. For most people, these questions no longer arise. Chinese and Singaporean education is admired around the world yet in these countries many young people are pushed by their parents and teachers to an extent unheard of in the West. 'Success' depends on results (particularly in science and mathematics) but in this supposed success something essential to what it is to be human is lost.

Charles Dickens (1812–1870) wrote *Hard Times* as a critique of crude utilitarianism and a fact-based approach to education, but with human beings increasingly being regarded as 'human resources' to be managed and used for the purpose of maximising profit, the lesson has hardly been learnt. The advent of Artificial Intelligence will, for millions of people, take away from them the possibility of a world of work, and meaning will then come to be found solely in entertainment. The evidence of this is already all around us with the relationship with the smart phone being more addictive and more important than any human relationship. Indeed, human relationships are increasingly mediated through the smart phone.

Materialism and consumerism foster this and contribute to the denial of any broader questioning about whether life has any meaning or purpose. The main hobbies today are sport, shopping and the media. Sport has always been a way in which the rich can subdue and distract the masses from the games of ancient Rome to the obsession with sport in many parts of the world today. Instead of past identity being found in tribal loyalty today it is all too likely to be found through the sports team a person supports.

Even more important than sport is the enslavement (and this is not too strong a word) achieved through the carefully cultivated obsession with shopping as well as desiring, acquiring and owning 'things'. Advertising and capitalism generally promote this, and the message given out in almost all media is that buying and acquiring things is the road to happiness. This starts very early on with children's television and the constant advertisements that occur on most channels. People are no longer valued in terms of who they are but in terms of how they are perceived, and this perception is not just based on personal appearance but on who owns what – whether this be house, car, barbecue, wife, husband, children or other accoutrements which are seen to be the marks of success. Plato was right – most people live in a world of shadows and do not want to confront anything that challenges the shadow world which they take to be so real. The Islamic poet, Rumi, put it very well:

These spiritual window-shoppers,
who idly ask, "How much is that?" Oh, I'm just looking.
They handle a hundred items and put them down,
shadows with no capital.
What is spent is love and two eyes wet with weeping.
But these walk into a shop,
and their whole lives pass suddenly in that moment,
in that shop.
Where did you go? "Nowhere."
What did you have to eat? "Nothing much."

Even if you don't know what you want,
buy 'something', to be part of the exchanging flow.
Start a huge, foolish project,
like Noah.
It makes absolutely no difference
what people think of you.
("We Are Three", *The Mathnawi*, VI, 831–845)

Dr Felicity McCutcheon, a leading Australian educationist, speaking at the 2002 Dialogue Australasia conference said that young people are continually told:

Follow your dreams, and
Make a difference.

But they leave school having no idea at all what this means or what to do. Schools are no longer interested in education – meaning bringing out human potential or even in discussing whether such potential exists.

This, then, brings us to a central issue which underpins the discussion of Truth and that is the question of the meaning of human existence. There is, again, a truth at stake:

1. Either life has meaning that we can discover and attempt to live out and this is directly related to human fulfilment.
2. Or we are simply advanced animals that create meaning before our short lives come to an end.

Deciding between these two is not just a matter of opinion. There is Truth a stake. It is this issue that has perplexed and engaged philosophers and seekers of wisdom since the dawn of recorded time and it is still relevant today although most people do not even consider it. Is our sole aim to be as happy as possible, and to minimize pain and any form of physical or mental suffering until we die?

This issue is becoming increasingly important with advances in genetic engineering made possible by CrispR. CrispR (Clustered Regularly Interspaced Short Palindromic Repeats) is a gene editing tool which acts like molecular scissors enabling 'faulty' genes to be repaired or replaced or new genes to be inserted into an early stage embryo. Once a human sperm enters the egg the chromosomes align and then start to replicate. At this early stage of development the cells are 'totipotent' – they can develop into every cell in the eventual human body. After about ten days specialisation begins and cells become pluripotent – this is the stage of stem cells. These cells can still develop into a more restricted range of organs, tissues, bones or cells. It is at the earlier, totipotent stage that real change can be achieved as if any cell is changed at this stage the duplication process will mean that every cell in the body is affected.

CrispR provides the prospect of being able to cure diseases or to enhance particular human characteristics. Scientists already believe they have isolated the genes for intelligence in mice, and it may not be long before prospective parents can choose to enhance their children's intelligence, sporting abilities or appearance. They may also choose, of course, to eliminate future diseases, to enhance the embryos' immune system or to affect their behaviour as it is already established that much human behaviour has genetic links (cf. p. 115). This is not science fiction as already in Britain the Human Fertilisation and Embryology Authority has given permission for the genetic selection of embryos to ensure that particular defects are not present in the future child. CrispR takes this one stage further as it allows gene editing and not just embryo selection.

The cost of CrispR is coming down but it is hard to foresee a future when all prospective parents who could benefit will be able to afford it. As a rule, genetic technologies are very expensive – they involve not just the scientists' but doctors' time and, increasingly, parts of the human genome have been patented and this will add additional costs. IVF/IVM remains expensive and CrispR will be far more costly. Assuming that CrispR, or a successor technology, were to become a safe, accepted embryo-editing technique, it seems almost certain that only the wealthy would be able to afford it leading to a genetic apartheid. Jim Kozubek said that, "these treatments will be available to only the wealthiest among us who can pay for them." This will have enormous consequences for humanity – already the gap between the wealthiest members of society and the rest is higher than it is has ever been and this trend seems certain to continue. The search will be on for genetic perfection and this, it is increasingly clear, means physical perfection. This will be a by-product of the dehumanising process that the new technologies may make possible.

The Transhumanist Movement is gaining ground with full-time professors now being appointed at major universities. It aims to improve future human beings either through using genetic engineering techniques or by combining these with cyborg technology. There is now clear evidence that some (by no means all) forms of depression have genetic causes. There is even stronger evidence that some people have a genetic disposition to violence or to addictive behaviour. If the aim of life is to be happy, then transhumanists make the case for genetic engineering of human embryos to ensure that they do not carry the gene that leads to depression, violence, addiction or other 'defects'. Similar arguments are made for genes linked to many diseases including some forms of cancer. This process of seeking to control behaviour as well as physical aspects of being human is certain to continue and accelerate – but it raises important questions.

What is it to be human? The issue matters and there is a Truth at stake which is closely connected to the claim that there is some form of transcendent or Eternal order. Every major philosopher whether they be theist, deist, atheist or agnostic has considered until very recently that this question is the most important one to answer, and its relevance is no less than it has been throughout the centuries. Today the question has been deliberately marginalised since, as everything is held to depend on opinion, there is no single answer. Truth is directly related to the nature of human beings and the question then arises as to how to understand this nature. To answer this, one needs to equip people with the tools to challenge conventional assumptions and to explore both the nature of argument and of reality.

Chapter Seven

The Nature of Argument and Reality

If ultimate Truth exists, how can it be found? Postmodernism is right that much depends on perspective, on culture, sexuality and gender, but may be mistaken to deny that absolute Truth exists. To dismiss the search for Truth without engaging in it rests on a prior assumption which may well be mistaken and, given its significance, has profound consequences. So how can Truth be sought? To address this, it is important to understand the basic nature of philosophic arguments. Traditionally there have been two types of argument.

Firstly deductive arguments which start from a general principle, a claim that everyone accepts, and then seek to derive other truths from this initial premise. These arguments are 'a priori' as they do not depend on experience as a starting point. An example might be:

1. Spinsters are female.
2. Georgia is a spinster.
3. Therefore Georgia is female.

If the first two statements are true, then the conclusion necessarily follows from it. Provided it is true that Spinsters are always female and that Georgia is a female, then (3) must be true. This type of argument is useful in mathematics or in analysing linguistic propositions but not in many other areas – not least because the truth of the first premise largely depends on the conventions of language. In our culture, 'Spinster' necessarily refers to a female and cannot refer to a male (although the situation becomes more complex when a person has mixed genders). 'Gay men are happy' was necessarily true in 1900 but today the word 'gay' has changed its meaning and so today the statement may or may not be true.

Secondly inductive arguments which are more useful and are the basis for arguments in science. These arguments are a posteriori as they are based on observation or experience:

1. Fish live in water.
2. This is a fish.
3. Therefore this lives in water.

The problem with all inductive arguments lies with the first premise. It one finds fish that live part of the time on land (as some do) then the argument fails. To take another example:

1. Every event has a cause.
2. The singularity is an event.
3. Therefore the singularity has a cause.

All that is needed is for one uncaused event to occur and the first premise is false. This gives rise to the problem of induction in science since, however many observations one makes, the next observation may falsify the general rule. 'All swans are white' was accepted as true until the first black swan was sighted in Australia. The second problem is that inductive arguments are essentially based on verificationism (p. 37). Their key premises depend on sense experience and if sense experience is not the best starting point, then this approach fails.

There is, however, a neglected third alternative type of argument and that is what the philosopher Charles Peirce (1839–1914) called abductive arguments. Abductive arguments start with observation and seek to show that the conclusion is the most reasonable hypothesis to explain the premises. Specifically, they do not rule out alternative conclusions.

Many scientific and medical proofs are abductive – they

seek to provide the most persuasive explanation given the data available. Occam's razor holds that the simplest explanation is the one to be preferred – abduction holds that 'simplest' can be defined as 'most plausible'.

The evidence for the singularity which occurred about 13.7 billion years ago explaining the origin of the universe is very strong. Many observations (including redshift, Fraunhofer lines, the background radiation from the singularity) seem to have confirmed this theory. Scientists generally accept the 'big bang' as it makes the best sense of the evidence currently available but there are dissenting voices proposing alternative theories – and these may become increasingly plausible. Medical diagnoses tend to be based, at least to some extent, on abductive reasoning. The doctor seeks as much information as is reasonable and makes an informed judgement – but the possibility of the diagnosis being mistaken is always there. Most doctors will recognise that, in any diagnosis, there are possibilities of rare alternative explanations for the symptoms that are presented.

Sometimes in science there is a need for a creative leap of imagination to arrive at a hypothesis which it may then take generations to confirm and, even then, the possibility of alternative explanations may be open (the Higgs boson is a good example). Abductive arguments are based on an inference to the best explanation. The best explanation is the simplest and most elegant.

Charles Peirce introduced abduction into modern logic. Before 1900, Peirce treated abduction as the use of a known rule to explain an observation. For instance, if the grass is wet then it is a reasonable inference that it has rained. This remains the common use of the term 'abduction' in social science and artificial intelligence. In 1903 he modified his approach to claim:

A fact, C, is observed:
1. If state of affairs A were true, then C would follow as a

matter of course.

2. Hence there is reason to believe that A is true.

But A may not be true, there could be alternative explanations – for instance someone may have been using a sprinkler. It is a matter of probability and of assessment of alternative possibilities.

The difference between inductive and abductive arguments is not always clear. Both arguments are a posteriori – both are based on experience. Very broadly:

1. Inductive arguments are meant to provide a convincing proof.
2. Abductive arguments are meant to point to the most probable explanation whilst recognising that there are other alternatives that are possible.

It may be that in looking for Truth, abductive arguments are needed – and this is important because abductive arguments take into account a broader range of possible evidence than that which a verificationist would accept.

This brings us to the nature of reality and this is intimately connected with the nature of Truth. Most people assume that reality is material – everything is made up of matter, matter behaves according to fixed laws and, in principle, science will be able to provide a complete explanation of everything, this includes human consciousness, brain states and ethical behaviour. This, of course, buys into the modern atheist and materialist world-view which dominates today – and which could, of course, be right. It is, however, entirely plausible that it is mistaken or at least gravely inadequate. The evidence for its inadequacy comes from science itself and, in particular, our increasing understanding of the quantum world. It is now clear that reality as we take it to be is reality mediated through our senses which have developed to enable us to live in the world at our scale. If, however, we adopt a different scale (at the nanotechnology level or, even further down, at the Planck scale) reality is totally and utterly different.

The complex nature of reality was realised by the ancient Greeks. Democritus argued that the universe is made up of invisible particles, but these are nevertheless finite. If they were of infinitely small size and could be permanently divisible then it would be impossible for them to ever come together to form matter so they must, he argued, be unbelievably small but nevertheless have some indivisible size (today we might think of it in terms of mass or energy). The whole of the universe is made up of the conglomeration of these particles. The Latin poet, Lucretius, wrote a poem "On the Nature of Things" which was influenced by Democritus' idea. Isaac Newton developed and built on Lucretius' insights (although how much direct influence there was is debatable), and argued for atoms being the fundamental matter of the universe which, he maintained, behaved in a mechanistic and predictable way – it was Newton who gave us 19th century science and the picture of a clockwork universe. Even more important, Newton discovered the effects of gravity and the force it imposes not just on objects on earth but on planets, moons and other celestial bodies. We now know, through Einstein, that the most basic level of reality is further down, at a far more fundamental level. They were all, nevertheless, right in showing that reality is not the reality that we experience every day.

Immanuel Kant recognised this with his distinction between the phenomenal world, the world as it appears to us through our five senses and which, he argued, is the only reality that we can know, and the noumenal world. The noumenal world is reality as it really is, independent of our senses and, for Kant, this level of reality is fundamentally inaccessible as our senses are not capable of accessing it. For Kant the 'moral law within', human freedom and aesthetics are all grounded in the noumenal world. They are profoundly real but unprovable through sense experience.

The advances in science and mathematics (and the two are linked) in the 20th century have given us a greatly increased understanding of reality at the most fundamental level. It is now clear that, instead of atoms being the fundamental indivisible 'stuff' out of which the universe is made, atoms are themselves far more complex. The carbon nucleus itself, so large and yet so unbelievably small, is surrounded by vast amounts of space. Indeed reality is mostly empty. Each carbon nucleus is made up of six protons and six neutrons. There are protons, neutrons and electrons in every nucleus out to the furthest galaxy. So, it might be thought, electrons are now the fundamental level of reality, but even this is inaccurate as electrons do not exist as fixed and stable entities. Instead there are myriads of potential electrons – and the word potential is important. These are not electrons, they are potential electrons. Reality at the most basic level is a vast ocean of potential existence which it is impossible to measure since the very act of measuring or observing an electron changes it (as the famous 'double slit' experiment demonstrates). Even electrons are no longer the fundamental nature of reality, and new particles and forces are being discovered every year.

Mathematics points to there being at least nine dimensions, perhaps more. Reality as it appears to us is the everyday world of trees, cars, people, dogs, pigs, aeroplanes, roads, stars, shadows and everything we take for granted. This is the phenomenal world – the world of phenomena observed through our senses. The noumenal world is the world as it really is independent of our senses and this is largely unknowable. There is a sense in which our senses are a prison – they have evolved incredibly successfully to enable us to live in and dominate our environment. They provide us with all the information we need for everyday life but they deceive us into thinking that this is the same as reality.

'Reality' is largely unknowable – indeed the evidence for the existence of dark matter (which is inaccessible, and which is held to make up a large proportion of the universe) just shows the growing chasm of ignorance we have about the most basic level of reality. We are like children playing on the shore of the vast ocean of potential existence and potential reality. It may well be that there are an infinite number of universes and, some scientists suggest, new universes may be coming into existence all the time. There are many theories but there is nevertheless a Truth at stake.

Abductive arguments require us to consider a wider range of evidence than that simply derived from sense experience since we now know that relying on sense experience alone will give us an incomplete and partial view of the universe. We think that truth is only to be arrived at through measurement – and measurement is the basis for most of science. The impossibility, however, of measuring electrons is but one example of the failure of measurement to provide a complete picture. This insistence on the necessity for measurement derives directly from verificationism (p. 37) and results in an essential reductionist approach to anything that cannot be measured. Similarly, ideas in the realm of aesthetics, morality, love, religion or other areas are reduced to ideas that can be measured – hence the rise in disciplines such as psychology and sociology. Sociology (cf. pp. 31–33) seeks to show the function of, for instance, religion, love and beauty in society – but the assumption that such functional explanations can provide a complete account is seriously flawed. The same applies, for instance, to human consciousness which we really have not begun to understand – the result is that we liken consciousness to computational power of the sort found in advanced AI. Once again, this is a reductionist approach.

Some will reply by saying that we can now measure human brain waves and even tell what people are thinking which indicates that brain waves and consciousness are the same thing. People can, indeed, communicate by thought waves. This does not, however, come close to explaining consciousness and it may be that our understanding of human brains is radically inadequate. Brains may function as quantum computers and, through quantum entanglement, may be able to behave in ways that we do not begin to understand. It clearly is inadequate to simply regard brains as a series of complex neural pathways. It is far more complex than that.

We are now forced to accept that Plato and Kant were right – reality as we take it to be is only reality as it is perceived by us. We are prisoners of our senses and, like most prisoners, we consider the walls of our cage to represent the totality of reality. This is far from the case. If we are going to produce an argument that gestures towards Truth we need to recognise that material science alone will provide only partial answers.

In the book *Flatland* (*Flatland: A Romance of Many Dimensions* by Edwin Abbot, 1884) and the subsequent film of the same name, a two-dimensional world is portrayed. All the beings in this world have only two dimensions, they have no idea of height. The beings were of different shapes – triangles and circles, rectangles and octagons. They move around on the flat surface in which they live. If a sphere comes into their world they would only recognise it as a dot where the sphere made contact with their flat reality. In this world one of the beings called 'Arthur Square' became convinced there was a third dimension. He was ridiculed by everyone and finally put on trial for heresy because he believed in a dimension which no one else accepted. In his trial he appeals to mathematics, to reason, to imagination and to a sense of wonder as pointing to a third dimension. We are in a similar position today, trapped in a material world which we take to be reality. This is precisely the situation portrayed by Plato in his myth of the cave (p. 17).

If there is an Eternal or transcendent dimension (as Plato

and many philosophers since have maintained) then it will not be accessed through normal science and it is precisely the paradigm of normal science that is now breaking down. Any argument, therefore, that seeks to apprehend Truth is going to be an abductive argument – an argument that persuades us towards a true understanding of the nature of reality when our senses have educated us into a reality we now know to be partial, limited and inadequate. Abductive arguments are the only way, therefore, of approaching an understanding of Truth and reality, and this requires us to take into account a much wider range of evidence than verificationists would accept.

The philosopher WK Clifford puts forward an analogy based on small creatures called trilobites which were closest to the beginning of life on earth. They lived between 600 and 300 million years ago at the bottom of the sea, and there are huge numbers of their fossils constantly being discovered. They were roughly between 1 millimetre to 70 centimetres long and shaped rather like a modern wood beetle. During this time they evolved from sightless creatures to develop eyes. Their fossils are readily available and can be bought on eBay. Clifford's story is as follows:

Once upon a time – much longer than six thousand years ago – the Trilobites were the only people that had eyes; and they were only just beginning to have them, and some even of the Trilobites had as yet no signs of coming sight. So that the utmost they could know was that they were living in darkness, and that perhaps there was such a thing as light. But at last one of them got so far advanced that when he happened to come to the top of the water in the daytime he saw the sun. So he went down and told the others that in general the world was light, but there was one great light which caused it all. Then they killed him for disturbing the commonwealth; but they considered it impious to doubt that in general the world was light, and there was one great light that caused it all. And they had great disputes about the manner in which they had come to know this. Afterwards another of them got so far advanced that when he happened to come to the top of the water he saw the stars. So he went down and told the others that in general the world was dark, but that nevertheless there were a great number of little lights in it. Then they killed him for maintaining false doctrines: but from that time there was a division amongst them, and all the Trilobites were split into two parties, some maintaining one thing and some another, until such time as so many of them had learned to see that there could be no doubt about the matter.

(WK Clifford, "The Cambridge Years", from *Such Silver Currents*, Monty Chisolm, Lutterworth Press, 2002)

The similarities with Plato's myth of the cave are clear. We are like Trilobites, the verificationists and materialists are those who assert that the reality we can experience and test is the only reality there is but the, few, outsiders will always call the remainder beyond this narrow and restricted understanding to a great appreciation of the nature of reality.

One of the main problems is that we are in a worse position than the Trilobites. Over millennia, they developed eyes and were able to progress in their knowledge and understanding of the reality in which they lived. Humans have traditionally understood that there was a broader dimension to reality and they sought this in religious categories which, as we have seen, were often inadequate and misleading. However, today the search for reality is being restricted as most people will only accept evidence that can be tested. They are like the majority of the Trilobites who refused to recognise that there can be a broader and more comprehensive approach to an understanding of the universe which includes all that science can offer but which cannot only be defined in scientific terms. Instead of being open to new ways of understanding reality, our minds are increasingly closed to anything but a verificationist mindset.

Over the centuries countless highly educated, intelligent and well-read people have affirmed the existence of mystical and religious experiences; near death experiences; telepathy; the existence of beauty in music, art, sculpture and other forms as well as the reality of Eternal values underpinning human ideas of justice, what is good and what is right as well as a broader understanding of reality.

Abductive arguments, as we have seen, do not seek to arrive at a conclusive proof. They instead claim to arrive at the most plausible hypothesis to explain the situation. Celebrity atheists argue for a materialist view of the universe which is devoid of meaning or purpose, and therefore will only accept truth claims that can be verified. Nevertheless they should (although all too rarely do) admit that they are arriving at a conclusion that could be mistaken and which disregards broader evidence which they dismiss. Those who argue for the reality of an Eternal dimension to life and that the universe has meaning and purpose are also putting forward what they see as the most plausible hypothesis. They, also, could be mistaken – but there is Truth at stake. Both positions cannot be true.

Chapter Eight

Explanation and Potentiality

If Truth is to be sought, then this is directly related to the nature of an explanation, and this is not straightforward. Often an explanation is an answer that we are satisfied with – but what satisfies one person may not satisfy another. A demand for a total explanation may be, in principle, impossible. Imagine an example: Assume a marriage has broken down and someone asks, "What was the explanation?" It is a common situation and the answers may be innumerable:

"She suffered from depression."
"There were too many money worries."
"He was impotent."
"He wanted children and she did not."
"The mother-in-law was a nightmare."
"He had an affair."
"She was too committed to her career."
"He was violent."

None of these explanations are adequate. Any one of them may or may not have contributed to the breakdown but the causes will be complex, varied, multilayered and may not be even partially understood by the parties themselves since they often reside partly in the psyche of the participants. In this type of situation, many people will lock themselves into a partial explanation and will see this as 'explaining' what happened. They will then live their lives based on this 'locked-in' viewpoint which may well colour all their family relationships.

In the film *The History Boys* a group of very bright students at a comprehensive school in a deprived area of Britain are hoping to get into Oxford University. No one from their school has ever gained entry to Oxford and they need to be coached so that they can understand the complexity with which Oxford University engages. Part of their education is to understand that truth in history is multifaceted and never straightforward, and any explanation will be filtered by culture and background. They want to put forward 'the explanation' for historical events that everyone around them accepts, and need to be brought to understand that this is inadequate.

Imagine someone asked for an explanation of you. How would you attempt to answer their question? Perhaps you might start by talking of the chromosomes that gave rise to your DNA and which resulted from the union of your mother's egg and your father's sperm, but would this be an explanation of you? Perhaps you might say that your behaviour, desires, sexual preferences and everything about you could be explained in terms of a detailed knowledge of your DNA – but few people would seriously consider that this would provide a total explanation of who you are. Faced with this sort of question, the idea of 'an explanation' is immediately seen to be inadequate and highly partial, possibly also grossly misleading. This is directly related to the issue of truth and we are often satisfied with a partial and incomplete explanation when this fails to account for a myriad of other facts – and, therefore, the 'truth' we are content with is only partial and incomplete.

The same issue applies when considering the universe. When asked, "What explains the universe," many might say "the singularity" which occurred about 13.7 billion years ago. This will, however, quickly be seen to be laughably incomplete as the precise conditions that gave rise to the singularity have to a large extent strongly influenced how the universe has developed, the science that we use to explain the universe and even the life forms to which it has given rise. To refer to just 'the singularity' does not begin to explain the complex interplay of gravitational chemical and physical forces that gave rise to the creation of carbon at the heart of exploding stars resulting from the nuclear fires generated by hydrogen and helium, and eventually to carbon-based life forms. Still less does it explain the possibility of human freedom and the effect that this freedom can have. It is appropriate, therefore, to consider the nature of explanation.

Aristotle was the most brilliant of Plato's pupils in ancient Athens. Aristotle was a Macedonian studying in Athens and since the Athenians and Macedonians never liked each other he was probably an outsider – not least because his approach to philosophy was very different from that of his teacher, Plato, and from most of his fellow students. He made one of the most significant attempts to deal with the issue of explanation.

Aristotle started by asking what the cause of a thing was, and recognised that no easy answer was possible. He analysed four different components when seeking to understand the nature of causation and, therefore, the nature of explanation. He considered that there were four elements to understanding the cause of a thing:

1. Matter: (*Physics* 11, 7, 194b24) This is what something is made of – but today this is not straightforward. Some people might say that everything is made of 'matter', but as we shall see what it means to talk of 'matter' is debatable. Newton thought that there were atoms at the fundamental level of reality but we now know that he was wrong. As we have seen, at the Planck scale there are not even electrons, there are only potential electrons. Reality is underpinned by a vast sea of potentiality. What is meant by 'matter' is a wide-open question.

2. Form, essence or inner nature: 'What it is to be' a thing of a particular kind. This is what the thing is or is to become. Today we might think of genetics. (*Physics* 11, 7, 194b27)

The 'form' or essence of a thing is what makes it what it is; it is effectively the arrangement of matter to make a thing what it is. 'Form' is, effectively, a blueprint. Raw matter has no 'form' at all, it is essentially chaotic – it needs 'form' to give it shape, to make it what it is. You cannot have matter without form or form without matter.

'The sensible form' is shown in the way it appears. Thus the sensible form of the moon is the way it appears to people. The moon, therefore, has the ability or potential to appear to people as a radiant disc in the sky. 'The form', however, is the essence of a thing – and this is much more complex. In the case of the moon, this involves an advanced understanding of the nuclear physics that lie beneath the reality of the sun which generates the light that is reflected from the moon and which makes the moon appear the way it is. It also requires an explanation of the craters on the moon, of the almost complete lack of an atmosphere, of a very small gravitation field as well as the forces that cause the moon to behave as it does. These explanations are not simply based on appearance; they require science, insight and considerable intellectual ability to even begin to understand the real form of anything rather than simply the way it appears.

One can express the difference between the 'sensible form' and the 'form' of a thing by saying that there is more to anything we perceive than meets the eye. This, again, returns the discussion to the nature of reality – gold may appear bright, shiny and (usually) gold in colour but this is only its sensible form. Its true form is only understandable at a molecular or subatomic level. Appearances can, therefore, be deceptive and only provide a partial account of reality and the nature of what it is to be a thing of a particular kind (whether goldfish, daffodil or wombat).

3. The efficient cause: 'Primary source of change' would be better – this is what brings about change. The father and mother are the cause of the form of the child, the potter the cause of the form of the pot. Forms are transmitted by, for instance, (a) sex, (b) by making things, or (c) by teaching. Aristotle is not thinking of cause and effect like we do. Change, for Aristotle, is the actualisation of potential. Clay has the potential to be made into a pot – but it needs a potter to actualise this potential in the clay. The actualisation of the potential to become a pot (and this potential lies in the clay) is the making of the pot by the potter. Teaching is a good example. Teaching is not something the teacher does – for Aristotle, it is something that happens in the learner. If nothing is happening in the student, the teacher is not teaching! The student has the potential to be taught, but if this potential is not actualised by learning taking place, then no teaching takes place. So efficient cause is the transmission of form, of what it is to be a thing.

4. The Telos, end or purpose: That for which something is done or made. Animals have feet in order to walk; a pot is made to hold water – these are their telos or purpose. The 'form' of a thing is the fully developed state to which everything strives, it is its final end of purpose. The telos of an acorn is to become an oak tree, the telos of a tadpole is to become an adult frog doing all the things that adult frogs do. Once a thing comes into existence (through the action of the efficient cause), then the telos (or end) of the thing will be the fourth cause – it will represent the purpose for which the thing was made. It seeks to fulfil the potential that is built into it. So:

    I. The pot is made to hold water (the maker transmitted this form into the clay).

II. The aeroplane is made to fly (the manufacturers transmitted this form into the assembled whole).
III. The rat has a nature that makes it behave as it does.
IV. A human has a certain nature and can fulfil its potential but its potential is determined by what it means to be human.

Everything strives to reach its potential – to fulfil the potentiality built into it by its nature. This applies to every animal and every plant and to the universe itself. The universe came into existence with the potential to develop stars, galaxies and planets as well as carbon-based life forms which can develop and fulfil their potential. These potentialities were latent in the very beginning of the universe, and when seeking to explain the universe these potentialities have to be taken into account.

For Aristotle, a key category in any explanation is potentiality. Everything that exists is actual in that it has existence but it also has potentiality to become what the nature of the thing enables it to become. A tadpole cannot become an oak tree, an acorn cannot become a swan. Something is good if it fulfils its potential – that is if it becomes what it has the potential to become. If something ceases to exist without fulfilling its potential (an acorn gets eaten by a pig, a tadpole gets eaten by a bird) then its potential is not fulfilled.

A human being has a potential to learn. When learning, one is actualising this potential – ignorance is replaced by knowledge. When the knowledge is used in practice, what has been learned is reinforced. Jonathan Lear in *Aristotle: The Desire to Understand* (p. 118) gives the following example:

1. Kermit as an embryo (bare potential – to develop into a tadpole, then into a frog, then into an active adult).
2. Kermit the tadpole (higher level potential to become a frog and then a mature, adult frog).

3. Kermit the mature frog – asleep (now fully actual at the first level as there is a fully actual, living body).
4. Kermit actively living his mature life now fully actualised not just as a body but using his capacities to communicate, feed, reproduce and interact with other frogs and the environment in which he lives.

If one accepts a limited or partial explanation as a complete explanation one will never approach Truth.

This leads to the central question – what does it mean to be human – and this is directly linked to the question of what it means to fulfil human potential. If we are going to explain the universe, the formation of stars and planets, the Higgs boson, DNA, natural selection, the incredible variety of plants and animals and anything else, this cannot be simply a matter of explaining their origins or how they work. To explain anything simply in terms of its origins would be far too narrow an understanding of the word 'explanation' – which is why Aristotle's analysis is so perceptive and relevant. It is necessary to answer much broader and more complex questions. Potentiality lies at the heart of these issues and, of course, it is contentious.

What is essential to recognise is that within the singularity which gave rise to the universe was the potentiality for there to be order, stars, carbon and, eventually, carbon-based life forms. All these potentialities were built into the initial singularity, and if the initial conditions are varied even fractionally from the incredible precision that gave rise to the universe, then no stars, planets or carbon-based life (let alone human beings) would exist.

In order to have life, it is necessary to have a number of chemical elements, the most important of which is carbon as this is necessary for long-chain molecules to form. The very early universe produced the two simplest elements – hydrogen and helium. These would provide a very uninteresting chemistry as little can be done with these elements alone. No carbon is made in the early universe, and there is only one place that carbon can be made and that is the interior nuclear furnaces of the stars. As the universe becomes lumpy and grainy, stars start to form and the nuclear processes then start. These nuclear processes make all the heavier elements that are necessary for life. One of the extraordinary achievements of astrophysics in the second half of the 20th century was to work out the processes by which this happened and is an extraordinarily complex and sophisticated process. It is only possible because the laws of nuclear physics take a very precise form. You need an incredible resonance of a particular form to turn three helium nuclei into a carbon nucleus. Professor Fred Hoyle of Cambridge University was the first to realise this, and he said that the universe is "an obvious fix", it's a "put up job". The improbability of the conditions happening by chance are simply too remote. Hoyle was a lifelong atheist and he did not like the word 'God' so he said that some capital I (standing for 'Intelligence') has monkeyed with the laws of nature. The potentiality for hydrogen and helium to form carbon in the nuclear fires of stars is part of the potentiality of the singularity, and one cannot explain the universe without taking into account this potentiality.

The second law of thermodynamics holds that entropy is irreversible and complex systems break down into less and less complex ones. The law of entropy, which governs all inert physical objects, maintains that any concentration of energy will dissipate, which is why ice melts and stars die. But life, including human life, is an anomaly, as it represents negative entropy. Living things increase their store of energy. There is no explanation why nature takes this route and reverses the Second Law. James Lovelock (the author of the 'Gaia hypothesis'), when he worked for NASA, was commissioned to determine what he would look for if he was looking for alien life forms and he concluded that negative entropy would be the best indicator of life. But since entropy is universal in the universe except where life is present, there is no explanation why the initial conditions of the singularity should have included the possibility of the reversal of entropy once life began. It is the very reverse of what might be expected.

James Lovelock has argued in a range of books that, in his words, Gaia (planet earth) "regulates" and "engineers" (his words) the conditions necessary for life. As a NASA scientist he has looked closely at the evidence over hundreds of thousands of years and has shown that:

> ... the entire range of living matter on Earth, from whales to viruses and from oaks to algae could be regarded as constituting a single, living entity, capable of manipulating earth's atmosphere to suit its overall needs with faculties and powers far beyond those of its constituent parts.
> (*Gaia: A New Look at Life on Earth*, p. 9)

Instead, therefore, of life being a random accident, Lovelock argues that Gaia itself engineers the conditions necessary for life. He gives a wide range of examples ranging from the oxygen content in the atmosphere (maintained at 21%, ideal for life), the salt content in the sea (maintained at 3.4% in spite of vastly greater amounts of salt being deposited in the seas over hundreds of millions of years), as well as the overall temperature of the earth (until it has been radically changed by human action leading to global warming). It is almost as though Gaia is a living entity able to respond to changed conditions. This is a quite extraordinary claim:

> The chemical composition of the atmosphere bears no relation to the expectations of steady-state chemical equilibrium. The presence of methane, nitrous oxide, and even nitrogen on our present oxidizing atmosphere represents violation of the rules

of chemistry to be measured in tens of orders of magnitude. Disequilibria on this scale suggest that the atmosphere is not merely a biological product, but more probably a biological construction; not living, but like a cat's fur, a bird's feathers, or the paper of a wasp's nest, an extension of a living system designed to maintain a chosen environment. Thus the atmospheric concentration of gases such as oxygen and ammonia is found to be kept at an optimum value from which even small departures could have disastrous consequences for life.

(James Lovelock, *Gaia: A New Look at Life on Earth*, p. 9)

The earth is the reverse of a product of random chance:

The keynote, then, of this argument is that just as sand-castles are almost certainly not accidental consequences of natural but non-living processes like wind or waves, neither are the chemical changes in the composition of the Earth's surface and atmosphere which make the lighting of fires possible. ... how does it help us to recognize the existence of Gaia? My answer is that where these profound disequilibria are global in extent, like the presence of oxygen and methane in the air or wood on the ground, then we have caught a glimpse of something global in size which is able to sustain and keep constant a highly improbable distribution of molecules. (p. 35)

All this potentiality was built into the initial singularity which increases still further the already astronomical odds of life evolving.

It simply will not do to say that the universe 'just happened' which is what the celebrity atheists claim. Faced with the incredible improbability of the conditions at the singularity being precisely right for the universe to form, and for carbon-based life to then evolve culminating in the development of life and eventually human beings, their answer is that no explanation is required. Richard Dawkins claims that extraordinary things do happen and the fact that we are here indicates that it happened and that is all that is required. This, however, is simply too inadequate. Every physicist will agree that the conditions necessary for there to be a universe at all, let alone for life to emerge, were so complex and so finely tuned that the improbability is beyond astronomic.

Professor Richard Swinburne of Oxford University likens the probability to being equivalent to ten packs of cards being simultaneously shuffled and all coming up with the ace of hearts. The odds of this happening are 52 (the number of cards in a pack) to the power of 10. This means 1 in 14,455,510,594,905,700. Such improbability demands an explanation and Aristotle would hold that all the potentiality of the universe had to be built into this initial explosion. To say 'it just happened' is a denial of science – and this has given rise to the alternative theory that there may be a near infinite number of universes (a multiverse) and we just happen to be in the universe where the conditions for stars, planets and life exist. This is, however, as much a faith claim as the claim that there is an intelligence behind the universe and Professor John Polkinghorne, one of the greatest quantum scientists of the late 20th century, argues that this is what drove him to accept the idea of an intelligence behind the universe. The really important point is that, whether or not this is accepted, one must acknowledge that the potentiality that was present at the singularity and that the incredible fine-tuning that made a universe possible requires an explanation. Science cannot provide such an explanation as it is precisely the existence of given laws of nature that provides the framework within which science operates – the framework itself is the province of philosophy and not science.

Polkinghorne argues that the introduction of the idea of

a multiverse is a desperate attempt to explain the incredible improbability of the singularity without bringing in the idea of God and that, even if there were a near infinite number of universes, this would not guarantee there was one that would create life. The example he gives is that there are an infinite number of even numbers but you will not find the quality of oddness within this infinite number of even numbers. So even a multiverse does not guarantee that there would be the conditions for stars to be created, for carbon to form and eventually for life to emerge.

Polkinghorne's conclusion is an abductive one (Chapter 7) and he argues that God is the most plausible explanation and the one with greater explanatory power than any alternative. If, he argues, one postulates God this enables one to explain a vast array of issues which otherwise would be improbable in the utmost extreme. It is a good scientific principle to accept the simplest explanation which accounts for the facts (Occam's razor), and God provides such an explanation.

If, as is undoubtedly the case, potentiality was built into the singularity (and even if one agrees with Dawkins and claims 'it just happened' the potential was clearly there) then this potentiality includes the existence of carbon-based life forms each with their developed individual potentialities as a result of natural selection and other factors leading to their respective species or nature. It is the aim of science to decide what this potentiality is. The potentialities of different types of animals and plants are reasonably easy to determine – one can arrive at these by a scientific study of how they behave. Atheists will, of course, maintain that essentially human beings are no different from animals and their potentialities can be discovered by simply looking at their behaviour. The question is whether this is adequate, and it is here that abductive arguments become important.

The idea that human beings have a distinct potential beyond

their essentially animal nature and that life has meaning and purpose will be rejected by many today as an outmoded notion with no modern relevance. Nevertheless this runs counter to deeply engrained insights in human nature as well as the insights of the greatest artists, poets, musicians and scientists down the centuries. It is also challenged by the sheer improbability of the singularity which points to some meaning, purpose and order in the universe which cannot plausibly be accounted for by pure chance.

The materialist, the atheist and the verificationist provide a convincing analysis but it is not enough. They refuse to question beyond what they see as a brute fact. Their explanation is essentially reductionist and moves from the claim that science can explain a great deal to the claim that their positions can provide a total explanation for reality. This is a faith claim as much as the faith claims of those, often although not always taking a religious standpoint, who claim that there is more to being human than a behaviourist and scientific analysis can explain. In particular, they cannot explain human potentiality just as they cannot explain all the potential latent in the singularity.

The position can be summarised as follows:

1) The singularity included all the potentiality to form Hydrogen and Helium, and then to form stars, carbon, planets and the whole universe.
2) This potentiality includes the conditions necessary for life to evolve and to sustain and develop life over millennia. The potential for natural selection is built into the singularity as well as all the processes to which natural selection gives rise.
3) This potentiality includes the potential to form human beings with all their immense diversity, complexity and yet similarity.

4) The incredible improbability of the singularity being precisely correct to enable stars and planets and the whole universe to exist is so great that it defies explanation and this means that, based on abduction, the simplest explanation is that there is purpose and meaning behind it.

5) If there is meaning and purpose then any explanation of what it means to be human requires us to go beyond a reductionist, materialist account. This will not adequately explain freedom (if this exists, which is a topic dealt with in Chapter 9), the aesthetic sense humans possess, the sense of empathy, creativity and love that goes beyond self-interest and a commitment to justice as well as the intrinsic value of every individual.

Point (5) is significant. What it means to explain human beings requires us to go beyond a purely behaviourist and physical account – these provide only a partial and incomplete explanation and, therefore, arrive at only a partial and incomplete truth.

Aristotle argued that if one was to understand the nature of any plant or animal then one needed to study them and, in particular, to study the best examples of their kind. If one wants to understand the full potential of a platypus one does not study those animals that are maimed or damaged in some way. The same applies to human beings. If one seeks to understand the true potential of humanity then one needs to understand the best examples and this will mean looking at their character, at the sort of person they are or have become over their lives. There are many examples but they might include figures like Jesus of Nazareth, Muhammad, Guru Nanak, Gandhi, Martin Luther King, Nelson Mandela, Florence Nightingale or possibly an old grandmother who, whilst not being academically able, nevertheless shows compassion, courage, gentleness, love and humility. Whether these factors are to be taken into account is, of course, a contentious issue. If these attributes are dismissed or simply explained in evolutionary terms then human beings can be explained in the same way as other animals. If, however, there is an 'Eternal' element in human beings (however this may be defined and this will be the subject of a following chapter) then more is required.

This, of course, raises the question as to which individuals are 'fully human', who fulfils human potential at its best. Some may say, "All human beings are fully human just by being alive." To accept this position means saying that Hitler, Himmler, Stalin, Pol Pot, Genghis Khan, mass murderers, rapists, and homicidal maniacs are just as fully human as the great saints and moral leaders down the centuries. In other words it means rejecting the idea that there is any such thing as human potentiality other than simply living, breeding and dying. When it is put like this, the absurdity is clear – there are obviously human potentialities that can be recognised across cultures. This is Aristotle's point and the same insight is recognised by all the great philosophers down the ages: Augustine, Ibn Sina, Ibn Rush'd, Rumi, Francis of Assisi, Thomas Aquinas, Moses Maimonides, Guru Nanak, John Stuart Mill, Immanuel Kant, Søren Kierkegaard, Barth, Bonhoeffer, Rahner and innumerable others would recognise there is something called 'being human' to which human beings can aspire. This is the basis for Virtue Ethics and for the Natural Law tradition of ethics – certain forms of behaviour draw us nearer to realising our full potential and other forms of behaviour diminish us and lead us away from this potential.

In a 1958 article Elizabeth Anscombe described how "Modern Moral Philosophy" had reached a dead end. Normative systems such as Natural Law, Kantian Ethics and JS Mill's Utilitarianism can seem to ignore what it really means to be human and live a good life in their focus on actions in the abstract. Anscombe argued that if there is no God, as increasing numbers of philosophers accepted by the 1950s, then even when Consequentialism, Kantian Ethics and Natural Law are formulated as secular approaches to moral theory, they are without proper meta-ethical foundations. They all use concepts such as 'morally ought', 'morally obligated', 'morally right', and so forth. These concepts are legalistic and, Anscombe argued, require a legislator as the source of moral authority. In the past God occupied that role, but in the modern world it is increasingly difficult to posit God as a necessary foundation for ethics.

In 1985 Bernard Williams developed Anscombe's idea in *Ethics and the Limits of Philosophy*. He argued that morality has become too concerned with abstractions, considering actions outside of their contexts, ignoring the different situations people find themselves in which affect their freedom and thus their responsibility. People are different and people develop; situations are different and they develop as well. This is key to the problem of moral luck, which Williams thought affects all traditional moral philosophy and makes systems unworkable. Bernard Williams argued that there is a need for a new approach to ethics, an approach...

1. Which looks at the bigger picture,
2. Which engages with the real world,
3. Which does not dwell on blame,
4. Which guides people towards a better life.

In 1985 Alasdair MacIntyre published the highly influential book *After Virtue*. Drawing on Anscombe and Williams (whose ideas were well-known before the publication of his book), MacIntyre reviewed the state of Ethics as a discipline and agreed that it had failed to provide useful guidance on how to live well. He saw the future in stepping back from any attempt to define rules or moral norms and in looking instead at the forms of behaviour which lead us to flourish and make positive decisions. MacIntyre acknowledged the difficulty in listing the virtues, given that they seem to change over time and between cultures; however, he suggested that the process of reflecting on what living a good life involves will, in itself, lead to moral improvement. However, there is, MacIntyre argued, a common core of what is understood to be virtue, which is consistent through time and between places.

A good person is always somebody who seeks to act with moral integrity, who reflects on situations and chooses to act on principle and consistently, fairly with respect of everyone. Aristotle owed a considerable debt to Plato in his ethical thinking, however, Aristotle was the first philosopher to study ethics as a distinct subject area. Plato discussed ethics as part of his broader political philosophy, such as in *The Republic*, and held a similar view on what a good life consists in to that later adopted by Aristotle, however, Plato did not move beyond listing qualities that a good man would have such as friends...

Aristotle recognised that there were differences of opinion about what a good life consists in. He argued that most people agree that it is good to do well in life, to be recognised by one's peers, to have friends, to have a family. Issues arise when people try to agree on which is the most important of these elements and which should take priority when it happens that a choice must be made. Aristotle tried to resolve these issues by clarifying the highest good, what must be the most important end for actions.

Aristotle is usually seen as the father of the Natural Law tradition, because he established the 'scientific' inductive approach which has come to characterize this approach to ethics. He argued that we can discover how people should behave by studying how people do behave; observation and rational analysis of human nature is the surest foundation for judgements about it. For Aristotle, Ethics are a product of practical reason, reasoning based on real-world experience. His word for practical reason is phronesis. For Aristotle, through observing successful human beings we can conclude that a fulfilled, flourishing or good human being is one who fulfils human potential and this particularly means cultivating the virtues. These have long been recognised across all societies although defining them is not straightforward – nevertheless they are grounded in the common human potential that all human beings share. Certain ways of behaving can draw individuals closer to realising their potential whilst others can debase the individuals concerned. There is an enduring wisdom here. Fulfilling human potential does not consist in buying things, owning things, in 'success', sex, happiness or reputation. It is directly linked to character and to what it means to be human. It is only by fostering the virtues, standing for what is good, right, just and true that human fulfilment can be found.

There is a 'more' to being human which is not easily defined but is nevertheless grounded in Eternal values. It is hard to explain, using only natural selection, why high human potentialities should have evolved as there seems to be no pressing need for them. Humans have been the dominant species for thousands of years and faced no real threats. Food supplies were generally adequate and the need for the virtues to develop and for a broader dimension of human potentiality to come into existence seems hard to explain on natural selection grounds. In the past, religious groups tried to explain this 'more' by arguing for a disembodied and non-material soul which was implanted by God at some stage after conception and which survived death. Plato and Socrates both saw survival of death as dependent on this idea of a soul. The early Christian Church fathers, not least Augustine, held to the same position and it was an early Christian heresy called 'Traducianism' to hold that a man and woman could mate and produce another human being. God, it was held, was needed to implant an immortal soul. Today many Christians no longer talk in these terms although Muslims do as the Qur'an specifically refers to Allah implanting a soul. Many people today, however, reject the idea of a separate soul but almost everyone still wishes to maintain that there is a 'more' to being human than a materialist would accept. Defining this 'more' is not straightforward but is directly linked to the virtues and to character development. The task of education should be to open young people's minds to the possibility of understanding there is more to life than acquisition of 'things' or what most people regard as 'success'. All these objectives are ultimately empty and will disappoint. Really good education is concerned with character development, with integrity, with compassion and with a search for Truth as well as living by Eternal values that are not transient. To put it more simply, it should be concerned with fostering 'good' people – yet this understanding of education is increasingly marginalised.

In order to explore how this 'more' might be understood, it is necessary to consider issues crucial to an understanding of human nature – which will include whether human beings are free and how to understand human potential.

Chapter Nine

Possibility and Necessity

The mating processes in all mammals are essentially the same. Whether it be mice, cattle, dolphins, sheep, rats, dogs, pigs, possums, wombats, chimpanzees or human beings the process is nearly identical. The male's sperm unites with the female's egg and after a gestation period the female produces between one and about twelve young. These young are then suckled until they are old enough to fend for themselves – the gestation period varies as does the period before the young become independent but there is very little essential difference between species. As we have seen (p. 47) Peter Singer argues that when conferring rights we are being speciesist if we give more rights to humans than to other animals simply because we maintain that humans belong to the human race and other animals do not. The idea that only human beings have 'natural rights' which are innate and which simply depend on species is, he claims, as outmoded as the idea that human life is sacred. Both are 'medieval' approaches stemming from religion which he considers to be outmoded and irrelevant in the modern world. What matters, he argues, is consciousness and the ability to make choices (p. 72).

The idea that there is anything eternal in human beings such as survival of death or a moral code that is in some sense linked to transcendent and absolute values is widely seen to be an idea whose time has passed. Morals, it is held, evolve over time and are based on reproductive success and the ability to foster the survival of the species. They are effectively based on a Hobbesian 'social contract' model which brings people to agree on a moral code as a basis for them being able to live together peacefully. This discussion has an impact on the debate about Artificial Intelligence. Just as the debate as to whether there is an ontological distinction between human beings and animals is important in ethics, so the debate about whether there is an intrinsic difference between humans and Artificial Intelligence is going to become more and more influential.

To hold that there is no essential distinction between humans, animals and AI is a persuasive position. It is not only in reproductive terms that mammals are essentially similar to humans – all seek to avoid pain and to exercise choices. It is true that the choices of most mammals are conditioned by their species and their genetics but the evidence in favour of this also applying to human beings is apparently strong. Evolutionary psychology (p. 57) seeks to explain human behaviour in genetic terms and Transhumanism (p. 115) looks to modify human embryos to maximise their future happiness and the happiness of the whole human community by, for instance, eliminating disease and behaviour that cause distress or damage either to the individual or to the community of which he or she forms part. Sociologists (p. 32) explain morality in terms of natural selection since those actions that foster society functioning well contribute to the success of human beings as a species.

Aristotle holds that human beings are distinct from animals as they are rational and have freedom. They may, therefore, choose not to fulfil their in-built potential as human beings. Animals have built-in potential and they will fulfil this potential provided food supplies are adequate, they are not killed by predators, accident or, perhaps, by weather or other adverse circumstances. The same applies to AI. Fulfilment of potential is not under the control of animals, plants or AI – they are programmed by their genes or by their computer code. The question is whether human beings are different since, some claim, they have the freedom to be able to choose whether to fulfil their potential or not.

This, today, is a contentious point. Perhaps human beings are indeed only advanced animals. As Richard Dawkins says, human beings may be the "robot vehicles blindly programmed by the selfish molecules known as genes". Humans are as programmed as a mouse, an alligator, a tree or, indeed, artificial intelligence. Natural selection may, it is argued, be capable in the future of providing a full account of what it means to be human, and the evolving discipline of evolutionary psychology will be able to explain all human behaviour in genetic terms. Freedom, it is claimed, is an illusion. This is not, however, necessarily the case.

What it means to talk of freedom is no longer clear. There are, broadly, three alternative positions:

a) Hard determinism argues that human beings are wholly determined. Freedom simply does not exist. Human beings may think that they are free but this is merely because they do not understand the evolutionary forces that determine us to act as we do.

b) Soft determinism or compatibilism argues for determinism but maintains that this is compatible with freedom. Human beings are free to choose how to act, but their choice is wholly determined. Freedom is then defined as the capacity to act in ways which we choose – even if the choice is determined.

c) Libertarianism. This argues for non-determined freedom and maintains that human beings can act as originating causes of action. This is an important idea. It means that human actions are not wholly determined by any previous state of affairs (whether this be genetic or cultural conditioning).

Most people want to believe that (c) is true, but the arguments in favour of (a) and (b) are strong. Unpredictable behaviour can be blamed on human ignorance of the causes of actions and the feelings they have of freedom may be argued to be an illusion based on a similar degree of ignorance about the forces that act on them.

One of the best examples of this position is given by David Hume:

> The vulgar, who take things according to their first appearance, attribute the uncertainty of events to an uncertainty in the cause... A peasant can give no better reason for the stopping of any clock or watch than to say that it does not commonly go right: But a scientist easily perceives that the same force in the spring or pendulum has always the same influence on the wheels; but fails of its usual effect, perhaps by reason of a grain of dust, which puts a stop to the whole movement...

> ... philosophers form a maxim that the connection between all causes and effects is equally necessary, and that its seeming uncertainty in some instances proceeds from the secret opposition of contrary causes... But the philosopher, if he be consistent, must apply the same reasoning to the actions and volitions of intelligent agents.

> The most irregular and unexpected resolutions of men may frequently be accounted for by those who know every particular circumstance of their character and situation. A person of an obliging disposition gives a peevish answer: But he has the toothache, or has not dined. A stupid fellow discovers an uncommon alacrity in his carriage: But he has met with a sudden piece of good fortune.

> I have frequently considered, what could possibly be the reason why all mankind, though they have ever, without hesitation, acknowledged the doctrine of necessity in their whole practice and reasoning, have yet discovered such a reluctance to acknowledge it in words, and have rather shown a propensity, in all ages, to profess the contrary opinion...

And it seems certain, that, however we may imagine we feel a liberty within ourselves, a spectator can commonly infer our actions from our motives and character; and even where he cannot, he concludes in general, that he might, were he perfectly acquainted with every circumstance of our situation and temper, and the most secret springs of our complexion and disposition. Now this is the very essence of necessity...
(David Hume: "The obviousness of the truth of determinism" from *An Enquiry Concerning Human Understanding*)

John Locke (1632–1704) gives the example of a man asleep in a locked room. The man thinks that he is free to leave the room, but in fact he is not. Hard determinists sometimes argue that criminals should not be punished for their actions as they could not do otherwise. They should, however, be locked up to protect society. Haeckel argued (1899) that everything (including thought) was the product of the material world (materialism) and controlled by its laws (causal determinism).

Hard determinism can be summarised as follows:

1. The whole world, including human beings, is made up of quanta in motion and this makes up matter.
2. The behaviour of quanta and matter is determined according to the physical and chemical laws of the universe.
3. Science can predict with reasonable accuracy the result of bodily interactions using the laws of the universe as a guide.
4. These predictions are largely accurate at microscopic and macroscopic levels.
5. Given the nature of quanta and matter there is no free choice. Physical matter cannot make free-will decisions at any level of organisation, especially the macroscopic (such as complex organisations of matter called human beings). All actions are determined by prior causes.

6. There is no such thing as moral responsibility, and morality is based on social convention and can be explained in evolutionary terms.

Hard determinists are called "hard" because their position is very strict; all events in the universe (including those initiated by human beings) are strictly determined. They are governed by inexorable necessity except in so far as random actions or genetic mutations may occur. In practice, the distinction between hard and soft determinism is not that great – both maintain that human actions are wholly determined but the soft determinist (or compatibilist) maintains that determinism and freedom are compatible.

Daniel Dennett is a modern compatibilist arguing that freedom and determinism do not contradict each other. Dennett argues that, because of chaos theory and other factors, human actions are always unpredictable – we can never know what human beings will do, hence there is room for apparent freedom. The stress is on the word "apparent". Although in the strict physical sense our actions are predetermined, we can still be free in all the ways that matter, because of the abilities we have evolved. Free will, seen in this way, is about freedom to make decisions without external compulsion, as opposed to an impossible and unnecessary freedom from causality itself. To clarify this distinction, he coins the term "evitability" as the opposite of inevitability – this is the ability of an agent to anticipate likely consequences and act to avoid undesirable ones. Evitability is entirely compatible with, and actually requires, human action being deterministic. Dennett moves on to altruism, denying that it requires acting to the benefit of others without gaining any benefit yourself. He argues that altruism should be understood in terms of helping yourself by helping others. Dennett seeks to undermine traditional ideas of 'freedom' and 'determinism' to show they can both be true at the same time. However, the freedom that he allows is only an apparent freedom – it is the appearance of freedom rather than, as Libertarians want to maintain, truly non-determined freedom.

Incompatibilists or libertarians are those who reject the compatibility of freedom and determinism. Such critics of Dennett argue that whereas the events that prompt human action may be random or indeterminate so far as the individual is concerned, Dennett's approach leads to the view that humans will act in totally determined ways in response to external or internal stimuli. They therefore want to maintain incompatibility between freedom and determinism.

The discussion can be illustrated by using a parallel with weather forecasting. There are so many variables involved in the weather and the systems are so complex that producing long-term weather forecasts is almost impossible. Nevertheless, an inability to forecast the weather does not mean that weather systems are in some sense 'free'; they are determined by a near infinite number of factors. Lack of predictability does not lead to freedom; it just means prediction is impossible – nothing more. Similarly with humans, we may not be able to predict precisely how they will act but this does not mean that there is some abstruse quality called 'freedom' which explains human actions. 'The weather' is not an originating cause of typhoons or sunshine, ice or snow nor are human beings originating causes of their action.

Whilst this picture is persuasive it suffers from weaknesses:

1. Weather systems are not conscious – human beings are. We do not understand consciousness (p. 58) – we have no idea what it means to be conscious. Advanced Artificial Intelligence may be able to perform incredibly complex tasks, it may be able to beat human beings at chess and to analyse a myriad of possibilities. Its behaviour may be able to match human behaviour in all important respects.

The 'Turing test' (p. 78) was designed to test whether the response of a computer or AI could match human responses so well that it was not possible to determine whether the response came from AI or from a human. However, this assumes that consciousness can be entirely analysed, without remainder, in terms of behaviour and this is simply false – the rich idea of an inner life with all the complexities that this involves is not susceptible to a behaviourist analysis. Lovelace put it well:

Stone walls do not a prison make,
Nor iron bars a cage:
Minds innocent and quiet take
That for an hermitage.
If I have freedom in my love,
And in my soul am free,
Angels alone, that soar above,
Enjoy such liberty.
("To Althea, from Prison", Richard Lovelace, 1642)

We constantly seek to devalue the place of human beings and to reduce them first to mere adjuncts in God's creative scheme and then to collections of atoms in Newton's billiard ball universe (as Niels Bohr is portrayed as saying in the film *Copenhagen*). We seek to be able to give a relatively simple explanation of what it means to be human, and reducing humans to being 'just' animals and consciousness to being 'just' measurable in terms of behaviour are both seeking a simplistic explanation which fails to capture reality. These claims simply will not stand up to modern scientific scrutiny – nor to the much more sophisticated understanding of causality argued for by Aristotle (p. 132). Consciousness (p. 58) may well be primary in the universe and not matter. 'Reality' is not simply material – at the most basic level there are not simply electrons – there is a vast ocean of potentiality, and consciousness can affect reality in ways in which we can only begin to vaguely understand.

2. Peter Singer (p. 47) is an atheist who sees human beings as simply advanced animals – there is no ontological distinction between species. What matters is rationality and the ability to make choices. Rights should be conferred on the basis of these abilities, and the rights of a dog or a dolphin may well be greater than a human baby or someone with Alzheimer's disease. Nevertheless, in arguing for the moral responsibility of human beings to take the suffering of animals seriously and, for instance, not to kill animals for food, Singer is effectively appealing to a standard of morality that is not simply based on evolutionary success. It is not simply a matter of the survival of the species which is what Darwinian natural selection suggests. The refusal to eat meat or the demand for a sense of moral responsibility to animals or the environment is precisely an appeal to a sense of morality which animals do not share.

The same argument can be applied to AI which, in behaviourist terms, will be capable of doing everything that human beings do. The question is whether a behaviourist analysis can provide a complete explanation of what it means to be human.

Libertarianism accepts that we are influenced by our background, genetics, etc. but argues that we are not wholly determined by these factors. There is a degree of non-determined freedom. Opinion may, of course, differ as to how wide this freedom actually is. This view is necessary for morality and for religion

– as non-determined choice is essential if there is to be moral praise or blame.

If the claim is made that human beings are morally responsible, then it is necessary for them to have non-determined freedom. If this non-determined freedom is denied, then so is moral responsibility. People may act wrongly, but they cannot be blamed for their action. The key issue is whether human beings are 'originating causes' of their action – this means that they originate (or have the capacity to originate) actions in ways which are not determined by internal or external factors. There is no way of proving whether, in fact, we have not-determined freedom. Whatever arguments are put forward in favour of humans being originating causes can be refuted. For instance:

1. "Each of us experiences freedom."
   REPLY: This just means we think we are free and it is our delusion that we are.

2. "To talk of temptation means that we know what it means to resist temptation."
   REPLY: Again this may be an illusion based on our ignorance of the forces acting on us – the fact that we think we can decide is simply mistaken.

3. "We make moral decisions and wrestle with the difficulty of these decisions – this shows that we have freedom to make these real decisions, otherwise the decisions would simply be delusionary."
   REPLY: Morality is based on social conditioning, and conscience is simply the values implanted in us by our parents. The idea that humans are originating causes is delusionary.

4. "People can surprise us, they can behave in ways that go

against all our expectations thus showing their freedom to not be determined."

REPLY: Of course people can surprise us – this is because we do not know all the factors controlling our behaviour or the behaviour of others.

5. "Human beings are not just made up of matter but there is a soul or spiritual substance which explains freedom."

   REPLY: This is a religious assumption for which there is no evidence and the postulation of a soul provides no explanatory power which goes beyond an explanation of brain states and genetics.

There is an exceptionally important issue here. If freedom is, indeed, an illusion then ethics, morality and religion are simply mistaken as freedom does not exist. Love does not exist except as a conditioned response to maximise breeding success, to overcome loneliness or to care for members of the same species with the aim, again, of fostering genetic success. Ethics then becomes a discussion of the processes by which human beings decide to live together founded on a Hobbesian social contract. There is no absolute standard of right and wrong (we are in the ethical post-truth world); instead moral codes develop as a result of natural selection processes to enable our genes to survive in an ordered society. Altruism can, for instance, be explained by human willingness to sacrifice immediate self-interest for the interest of the wider human group. 'Charity tends to begin at home', it is claimed, and this is because we are most inclined to be charitable to those who have some kinship or genetic relationship to us. The closer the relationship, the more altruistic we will feel. Cogent arguments can be presented to support this position but, in the final analysis, there is absolutely no way of determining whether or not it is true.

Immanuel Kant recognised the difficulty. He argued that there is no way to determine whether human beings have the capacity for non-determined freedom, but it is a necessary postulate of any ordered, moral universe. This does not, of course, make it true – all Kant is arguing is that iff (if and only if) the universe is fair and just then we must have freedom. The possibility nevertheless exists that the universe may be neither just nor fair but simply indifferent. Once again abductive reasoning is needed to arrive at this conclusion and opinions will differ as to whether it is true.

Philosophers who debate the issue of freedom tend to argue for one of the three alternative positions above but this may be a mistake. Perhaps freedom is not something that human beings have or do not have – freedom may be an achievement which can be hard won and is not easy to realise. Perhaps, as Plato argued, human beings are effectively slaves but have the possibility of achieving freedom (cf. p. 18). This means that they have the potential to achieve freedom in a way which animals or, arguably, AI does not.

Christians have long held the idea of original sin – this derived particularly from St Paul but also St Augustine. Augustine records in his diaries that he was looking out of his study one day and saw a woman breastfeeding twins, one on each breast. Whilst he watched, one of the babies finished the milk of its side and sought to push the other out of the way to get access to the second breast and its milk. This had a profound effect on Augustine. He had previously thought sin resided in the will, but clearly babies could not will to sin. As a Christian of his time, he took the Genesis story of the creation of the world relatively literally, and this records God creating the world and seeing it as good. How then, he pondered, could sin and evil enter a good world? The answer he found was in the disobedience of Adam and Eve in the Garden of Eden, and he therefore argued that all human beings are affected by 'original sin' which was passed down through their descendants. Christians today need to be uncomfortable with such an approach as almost every serious academic scholar considers the creation stories to be myths – stories that convey truth about the dependence of the universe on an intelligence without being literally true. The stories (there are two independent stories, dated, scholars consider, about 400 years apart; the earlier one runs from Genesis 2.4b to the end of the chapter, and the later from Genesis 1.1 to 2.4a) seek to show the dependence of the universe on God, and the human capacity for disobedience, and are not to be taken as literally true. Perhaps, however, there is a better way of understanding original sin.

If human beings have a capacity for freedom, then this capacity is continuously undermined by many factors not least upbringing, culture and personal desires. Human beings, like other animals, are born into this world and grow up surrounded by parents who teach them behaviour, morals and socialization. They develop in societies that value certain goals and aspirations. Almost always these goals are grounded in security, the acquisition of things, relationships, children and pleasure. The humanist psychologist Abram Maslow argued that humans have a hierarchy of needs starting with the need for security, shelter, food, warmth, sex and developing into needs for love and eventually self-actualisation. These needs are important for survival but preoccupation with them can form a prison from which it is exceptionally hard to escape.

Today capitalism has encouraged people to aspire to and find meaning in acquiring wealth, sexual activity, seeking to maintain youth, achieving financial and reputational success and thereby finding emotional and physical security. These are encouraged by advertising, the media and the dominant culture and, for many people in the West, shopping is a major hobby rivalled only by the Internet and addiction (and this is not too strong a word) to smart phones and the diversions they bring. The prison has grown even higher walls. Suppose that, however, as some of the greatest philosophers down the ages have argued, these are a distraction from the more fundamental goals of seeking freedom from these preoccupations. Naturally security is necessary for survival but there is a difference between recognising this and allowing a total preoccupation with these external goals to form a prison from which release becomes exceptionally difficult.

Kant argues that we are determined in so far as we are animals and conditioned by the material world, but our freedom lies in something beyond this – in the noumenal realm – and is based on reason. Kant argues that we are right to blame people for acting badly because they have failed to use reason:

One may take a voluntary action, e.g. a malicious lie... and one may first investigate its moving causes, through which it arose, judging on that basis how the lie and its consequences could be imputed to the person.

With this first intent one goes into the sources of the person's empirical character, seeking them in a bad upbringing, bad company, and also finding them in the wickedness of a natural temper insensitive to shame, partly in carelessness and thoughtlessness; in so doing one does not leave out of account the occasioning causes. In all this one proceeds as with any investigation in the series of determining causes for a given natural effect.

Now even if one believes the action to be determined by these causes, one nonetheless blames the agent, and not on account of his unhappy natural temper, not on account of the circumstances influencing him, not even on account of the life he has led previously. This blame is grounded on the law of reason, which regards reason as a cause that, regardless of all the empirical conditions just named, could have and ought to have determined the conduct of the person to be other than it is.

(Immanuel Kant, *The Critique of Pure Reason*)

For Kant, the child abuser who was himself abused must be condemned not because the childhood influences were not present but because, as a human being, he could have used reason to act otherwise than he did and this failure is itself a moral failure. Giving in to instinct caused by genetic or background factors is a denial of what is essential to our humanity – the ability to reason. Kant may, of course, have been too optimistic about the potential human beings have to exercise freedom. He himself was highly educated and from what we know of him tried to live a life dominated by reason. Many people are not well educated and have unfortunate (to put it mildly) home and genetic backgrounds, and it may be exceptionally hard for them to break free of their conditioning. In fact, whatever one's background and however fortunate one's education, breaking free from one's background can be exceptionally difficult and freedom may be something that few achieve. Nevertheless, to say that it is difficult is not the same as saying it is impossible. The road to freedom may well be a hard one that few are willing to travel.

Søren Kierkegaard argued that most people are, or feel they are, governed by necessity. They see no way out of the position they have arrived at and feel locked into situations over which they have no control. He argued that the opposite of necessity is possibility and the possibility of coming to freedom and breaking free from the chains that bind us so effectively is always present.

Clare Carlisle, writing in the British *Guardian* newspaper says of Kierkegaard:

In *The Sickness Unto Death*, the despair that lacks possibility is described as "spiritless philistinism", which both "tranquilises itself in the trivial" and "imagines itself to be the master". In our own world, this takes many different forms: the reduction of spiritual teachings to rigid dogmatism; the commodification of romance; the stifling of intellectual life by a fixation on measurable "skills", "outputs", and "impacts". In our universities, the threats currently posed to the humanities – and to Philosophy in particular – provide all-too-concrete evidence of this philistinism. Just days ago, for example, the University of Middlesex announced the closure of its thriving Philosophy department for "purely financial" reasons.

In such times, Kierkegaard reminds us that without possibility we are not fully human. The "choices" we hear so much about – which product to buy, which career politician to vote for – should not be mistaken for true possibility. (On the other hand, resistance to spiritless philistines, certain university managers included, remains possible.) If God is "that all things are possible", then the question of what it means to relate to God cannot be separated from the question of what kind of life we want to lead, and what kind of world we want to live in.

It is here that, once again, abductive arguments come in (p. 118). It is a matter of which is the most persuasive position, and opinions will differ on this. There is no empirical proof that we are not the programmed robots determined by our genes that Richard Dawkins claims we are, but there is also no proof that his position is correct. The walls of the cultural prison in which human beings live seem to impose a necessity on human life and behaviour. It may be that this necessity is a denial of the real situation – maybe the possibility of human freedom can enable choices to be made which undermine and negate the supposed necessity which rules out actions.

Rational analysis seems to point to human beings being determined by necessity and a good deal of theology makes the same point. In Islam, everything is held to be determined by the will of God, and many Christian thinkers (including Augustine and Calvin) have been determinists arguing that God predestines everything and the idea of freedom is an illusion. If this is the case, then human beings are essentially biological, determined robots with the determination coming from a great power figure who orders everything according to his almighty will. If this is the case, then rape, genocide, paedophilia and every other form of despicable activity are also ordered and determined. Such a position destroys what is fundamental about human beings and places them in the grip of a divine necessity.

If human life is to have any value at all then genuine, non-determined freedom must be achievable. It is this freedom that opens the door to possibility rather than necessity; it is this possibility that grounds hope rather than despair; it is this possibility that makes love more than a biological force; it is this possibility that provides grounds for faith rather than a descent into meaninglessness and it is this possibility that opens the door to the possibility of a response to the Eternal. In other words, freedom raises the possibility that there is something transcendent that human beings can strive to realise and to live by.

If human beings are free, then how can this idea be understood or explained? Partly this revolves around how a human being is to be understood. Classically there are two basic positions:

1. DUALISM – this maintains that human beings are made of two irreducible elements – soul and body. These two interact, and neither can be reduced to the others. On this view, real identity lies with the soul and not the body, and it is the soul that survives death. This was the position taken by Socrates, Plato, Descartes, Islam and traditional Christianity. The great advantage of this approach is that when a person dies their body rots or is burnt and nothing

remains – having a disembodied soul makes it possible to argue that the body is secondary and that true identity lies with the soul. Plato argued that the philosopher's greatest task was to care for the soul and not to act in ways that would damage the soul. In spite of its apparent attractions, there are considerable philosophic difficulties with the idea of a soul not least that there is no evidence for the existence of such an entity, and it is not clear what would be explained by postulating a soul which cannot be explained by an analysis of brain states.

2. MONIST MATERIALISM – this maintains that human beings are made up of one substance (hence 'monism') and this one substance is matter. Humans, like animals, are essentially material beings, and matter behaves according to laws that are, in principle, predictable. Most materialists tend to be atheists as there are severe difficulties with any idea of life after death if one is a materialist. If, on death, the body rots or is destroyed then life after death becomes an impossibility unless God or some other agency creates a replica of the person who has died with the same memories, brain states and possibly appearance. However, a replica is not the same individual as the one who died. There are very large numbers of replicas of the Magna Carta but none of them are actually one of the original copies of the Magna Carta. They are secondary copies.

These, then, are the two traditional ways of looking at what it means to be human. There is, however, a third alternative which originated in the 17th century in the writings of Bishop Berkeley, but has now acquired increased plausibility.

3. MONIST IDEALISM – this maintains that human beings

are made up of one substance, but this substance is not matter but consciousness. Consciousness is primary in the universe, and matter depends on consciousness not the other way round. At first glance, this appears ridiculous – of course, it will be asserted, matter is primary. The whole world around us is material. How can it possibly be seriously claimed that matter depends on mind or consciousness? The very idea seems ludicrous. We now know that at the most fundamental level of reality, the Planck scale, there is no matter. There are not even electrons – there are only potential electrons. The word "potential" is important. Reality is not made up of electrons but of a vast ocean of potential electrons which both do and do not exist, and which are impossible to measure since any measurement changes the potentiality and changes the electron. Reality at this level is no longer material – beneath the surface level of matter with which human beings are familiar is, therefore, a unified field of potential existence. We are a manifestation of this universal field.

Heisenberg's uncertainty principle is a central discovery of subatomic particles. Where a particle is and where it is going (its position and momentum) cannot be precisely pinned down. However, fundamental particles are entangled – one will affect another even though they are at opposite ends of the universe in a process which we do not understand. Quantum entanglement is the suggestion that these fundamental particles can be entangled with others. If the human brain functions as a quantum computer (as has been suggested by Professor Dean Radin, Professor Hameroff and others) then the possibility exists that there could be a quantum equivalent of the brain which could explain out of body experiences, telepathy and even possibly life after death. The evidence for this position, as yet, is meagre but there are significant scientists who hold it to be true. If (and this is, admittedly, a big 'if') it is true, then human freedom could be explained as at the quantum level the laws of matter no longer apply. If consciousness is primary, the materialist view of the universe breaks down.

We really do not understand the nature of reality – the more we understand, the more we realise just how very, very little we do understand. What we do know is that the Newtonian idea of a 'billiard ball' universe based on material laws is radically incomplete. It operates at our level of reality, but certainly not at a deeper level. All we can say is that the breakdown of classical materialism has opened the door to possibilities of understanding human existence that were simply undreamed of even fifty years ago. We no longer know what 'matter' is, what 'reality' is or what it means to be human. This opened conceptual space for artists, poets, painters and religious people to claim insights into the nature of humanity that can no longer be simply dismissed. If matter is no longer primary, then determinism seems increasingly unlikely and the potential (that Aristotelian word again!) becomes a real possibility. It may still be something that can only be achieved by great effort to break through the chains of culture conditioning, but the possibility is still there.

PJ Kavanagh (*The Perfect Stranger*, Fontana, 1985, p. 139) says:

The moment I'd been waiting for had arrived and it's difficult to describe precisely, or without sounding pretentious, but it comes quite clearly to a certain temperament (I can't speak of others) and presents itself as a choice; is one to live by one's own selection of realities, or that of other people? It can be crudely represented (to avoid talk of leaps into abysses and walks into darkness which nevertheless might contain some truth) by the decision whether to jump on an escalator (the existence of which is in exact proportion to your belief in it) or simply to approach the normal stairs in the normal way, one at a time, pausing and looking. It is in fact a move into the dark for the sake of a possible greater clarity – a gamble. Prudence suggests the jump may be into thin air. Faith, that's to say the trust that places foremost those sudden unclenchings of the heart and nerves, infrequent maybe but nevertheless glimpses of a world of possibility in which reality can be re-arranged, within the same limitations, say, as those of a landscape gardener – faith in those redeeming revelations (there are no other words for them) demands that you jump. Really, it depends what sort of world you prefer, and perhaps there's only an illusion of choice. But there is nothing illusory about the moment. I knew perfectly well I was deciding the course of my life, not only in the practical sense, but also the course of my future being. What I had to decide was whether or not I believed enough in the existence of what I wanted.

Being fully human means accepting and striving for the possibility of freedom and then being willing to use this freedom to live in a different way. This is a negation of necessity and opens the door to possibility. Faith involves a commitment to possibility, hope involves a commitment to possibility. Despair involves accepting the inevitability of necessity, a denial of freedom and, thereby, a denial of hope. Helen Keller said that, "Optimism is the faith that leads to achievement. Nothing can be done without hope and confidence." It is hope, optimism and possibility that holds on to the claim that the universe has meaning and purpose, that human life is significant, that there is an absolute distinction between what is good and evil, between living in some ways rather than others.

This possibility is not open to animals or indeed, it may be argued, to even advanced AI. Possibility opens the door to an ontological distinction between humans and other biological or artificial life forms. For human beings to be capable of defining themselves not in terms of their culture or their peers but to be capable of marching to different music is a radical possibility and it negates the necessity which many people consider constrains them. The possibility exists to engage one's life – not simply intellectually but with one's whole being, and this does not depend on financial, reputational or material success: To renounce the world's way of looking at things and make a commitment to things unseen, unproven but hoped for in the knowledge that one could be mistaken. It may be that only by so doing can one begin to understand the incredible richness of what it can mean to fulfil human potential.

Truth about the human condition, therefore, revolves around what potentiality lies within human nature. The materialist will confine his or her study to psychology, sociology and anthropology, and will seek to explain human behaviour in clearly defined terms. It will largely revolve round a well-functioning society and 'happiness' (whatever that means) and the avoidance of pain. The idea that there is a broader range of human potential grounded in the possibility of freedom and living according to a different set of priorities maintains that there is more to life than that.

Chapter Ten

Truth and Religion

If human potentiality goes beyond any animal or AI potential, if Absolute Truth exists, if an Eternal dimension to reality has any meaning or relevance, then religion should be at the heart of its affirmation. In a world dominated by verificationism and materialism, in a post-truth, relativistic and nihilistic world, religion should be the voice that provides the clearest challenge and clarity. 'Religion', however, in the Western world has become so hollowed out, so denuded of meaning or significance that whereas it once spoke with a relatively clear voice, it now tends to mumble platitudes and is easily ignored. The idea of a 'God in the sky' laying down seemingly arbitrary commands and punishing people for all eternity is simply no longer credible. Religions have endorsed war, persecution, slavery, economic injustice, the suppression of women, oppression and sometimes sadistic violence all in the name of an unseen power figure whose prime requirement seems to be the demand for unthinking obedience. Such a picture is readily adopted and developed by religious institutions who use such an approach to back up their own claims to power, authority and control. The religious imperative can easily be subverted to become a form of nationalism, racism, greed, power, ambition or narcissism, and there are few counter forces to question their authenticity. For many in the West 'religion' has, rightly, become irrelevant.

The radical voices of the founders of the great religions have been silenced in favour of a deadening conformity and mediocrity or through the use of religion as a power mechanism (as Karl Marx rightly recognised). Instead of a concern for the poor, the weak and the vulnerable religion has too often been used to bolster and enhance secular power structures. This does not mean that the radical voices of the founders of the great religions have been shown to be irrelevant or have been disproved, just that religion has often become an empty vessel, a sounding board often providing no resonance or content. The sexual abuse scandals, the multiples of different interpretations, traditions and denominations each certain that they alone have the truth, the focus on rules and rituals rather than essential content, the abuse of power and misogyny have meant that the voice of the Eternal has become almost silent. The question 'Where is the Eternal is to be found' can seldom today be answered in terms of religious institutions.

In CS Lewis' book *The Screwtape Letters* an older devil speaks to a young devil and says that their victory is assured once people no longer believe that they exist. In many ways, religion has become the greatest enemy of 'The Eternal'. Nowhere is this more the case than in the field of education as many religious leaders and the denominations that they represent are far more interested in a programme of catechetical indoctrination (and that word is used deliberately) rather than in helping young people think deeply about central questions of meaning, value and purpose. The result is that most religious education in the West succeeds in inoculating young people against religion and the search for the Eternal becomes irrelevant. The nascent quest with which young people are endowed (in terms of a sense of wonder, beauty and a broader appreciation of reality) is extinguished by the very organisations that should be supporting the quest.

In some parts of the world, religious education requires little thought or intellectual engagement and is primarily concerned with memorizing a text that is regarded as sacred, in others it is a matter of participation in rituals and understanding symbolism and creeds. In the West, in some religious schools, entrance requires parents to demonstrate that the children go to Church regularly in order to be considered – the result is that, through gritted teeth, parents all too often force their reluctant children to attend Church each week knowing that this is the price they have to pay to gain entry to schools that are regarded as desirable. Their attendance often has nothing to do with genuine belief or commitment; it is a means to an end. The children realise this all too well, and in most cases cannot wait to stop 'going to Church' as this is what 'religion' has come to mean. If someone is asked whether a person is 'A good Catholic' or 'A good Christian'; if they are asked whether they are a faithful Jew or Muslim this will generally be taken to be asking whether they regularly attend Church, Synagogue or Mosque. This is to miss the point.

Even where religious education is undertaken in an academic and neutral manner, it is largely a matter of rational evaluation or understanding the background to beliefs systems and practices within diverse traditions – all of which helps to reinforce relativism and the view that every culture has different practices. Essentially the approach is sociological. This encourages the new god of tolerance which is widely worshipped, but tolerance (whilst admirable) masks relativism and leads many young people to see religion solely in historical or sociological terms. Tolerance and relativism are not the same yet they are too often conflated. This is not to say that good religious education does not occur but it is all too rare.

The two dragons with which this book started are both at work in the field of religious education. On the one side is indoctrination which refuses to accept an intellectual and critical approach which allows young people the freedom to think for themselves, and on the other side is a reductionist, sociological approach. England used to be one of the leaders of the world in religious education but this is no longer the case. In July 2018 a government-commissioned report was produced recommending an essentially sociological approach which was devoid of theological content. Bishop Marcus Stock, the lead Bishop for religious education for the Catholic Bishops Conference, rightly condemned the report as essentially sociological, but the alternative is not a catechetical approach which smacks of indoctrination but rather a methodology which allows young people to engage in an open-minded search for meaning, understanding and Truth.

If the above paragraphs seem harsh, they are nevertheless realistic and the challenges are understood by some at least of the very highest level of the Christian Church. The Jesuit Journal *La Civiltà Cattolica* is so close to the Vatican that the Pope's Secretary of State has to approve all the articles published. The editors are known to be very close to Pope Francis. In July 2017 this journal produced an incredible editorial attack on neoconservatives in the United States who have brought together conservative Catholics and fundamentalist Protestant evangelicals to preach what is effectively a gospel of hate. It condemns: "Manichaean language that divides reality between absolute Good and absolute Evil" and the "stigmatization of enemies who are often 'demonized.'" It accuses fundamentalists of using scriptural texts out of context to give theological justification to belligerence as they prepare for "Armageddon, a final showdown between Good and Evil, between God and Satan." These fundamentalists falsely portray ecologists (of which Pope Francis is a leading figure) as people who are against the Christian faith. The editorial condemns the proponents of 'prosperity theology' that promises wealth to God's followers. This attack is extraordinary. Here we have a journal very close to the Pope challenging, in very clear terms, the way that Catholicism and evangelical Christianity have been hijacked by those in power to suit their own interests. 'Religion' has become, as it has so often been in human history, an enemy of the Eternal and the transcendent.

Timothy Kirchoff writing in *Ethika Politika* in January 2014 (republished in July 2017) said:

In *Evangelii Gaudium* paragraphs 93–97, Pope Francis lays

out two forms of "spiritual worldliness" that he views as obstacles to true Christianity. A comparison of these passages with what... Joseph Ratzinger saw as the future of the Church suggests that the (present) Pope and the Pope Emeritus (the previous Pope) share a vision of what the Church will need to become in the years ahead. The things that stand in the way of the church Ratzinger envisioned are precisely those that Pope Francis identifies as problematic.

Cardinal Ratzinger (later to become Pope Benedict XVI), writing at the end of the 1960s, seems to predict the total collapse of cultural Catholicism and the institutions that characterize it:

> From the crisis of today the Church of tomorrow will emerge – a Church that has lost much. She will become small and will have to start afresh more or less from the beginning. She will no longer be able to inhabit many of the edifices she built in prosperity. As the number of her adherents diminishes, so will she lose many of her social privileges. In contrast to an earlier age, she will be seen much more as a voluntary society, entered only by free decision.
>
> And so it seems certain to me that the Church is facing very hard times. The real crisis has scarcely begun...
> (*Faith and The Future*, Ignatius Press 2009, chapter, "What Will the Church Look Like in 2000?")

The Church, Ratzinger predicted, would lose its social prestige and many of its institutions. Compare this prediction with Pope Francis's condemnation of the form of spiritual worldliness that he calls Gnosticism:

> This spiritual worldliness lurks behind a fascination with social and political gain, or pride in their ability to manage

practical affairs, or an obsession with programmes of self-help and self-realization. It can also translate into a concern to be seen, into a social life full of appearances, meetings, dinners and receptions. It can also lead to a business mentality, caught up with management, statistics, plans and evaluations whose principal beneficiary is not God's people but the Church as an institution.

(*Evangelii Gaudium*, p. 78)

Cardinal Ratzinger said that: "sectarian narrow-mindedness as well as pompous self-will will have to be shed." The obsessive adherence to a "particular Catholic style from the past" and inquisitional analysis that Pope Francis has criticised can easily fit under the label of sectarian narrow-mindedness. Similarly, pompous self-will is evident in the mindset of those who, in Francis's words, "would rather be the general of a defeated army than a mere private in a unit which continues to fight."

In many Churches the main preoccupation is money and finance in order to keep the buildings maintained and 'the enterprise on the road'. If one looks at the great Cathedrals of Europe, the main concerns of the Deans and Chapters (or their equivalent) is often maintaining the fabric of the building rather than bringing people to any appreciation of the Eternal and the demands it makes. Much time and effort are spent in discussing fund-raising initiatives and limiting spending on anything that is not regarded as 'relevant'. Real education about human potentiality and a transcendent dimension to life is often regarded as a sideline. Often a preoccupation with music as an end in itself or in attracting numbers (which means generating greater income) is seen as the primary focus. This is not, of course, to undermine the importance of music as a door to the transcendent but it should, at least in a religious context, be a means and not an end.

In spite of the increasing irrelevance of religions in the modern

Western world, they have traditionally stood firmly behind the claim that Truth matters – perhaps more than anything else. The Hebrew Scriptures talked of the importance of wisdom, the word occurs 247 times in the Hebrew Scriptures, and there are 47 references in the New Testament. Although in Genesis 3.6 Eve is portrayed as being tempted by the fruit that would bring rational understanding (although this might be understood as seeking 'cleverness' rather than wisdom) and in some of Paul's epistles human wisdom is portrayed as empty in comparison to God's wisdom, in almost every other case there is praise for the search for wisdom.

Solomon asked God for wisdom and because he asked for this gift God gave him all those things for which he did not ask. Job links age with wisdom and understanding and sees wisdom as being a defining characteristic of God – in fact Job rejects his so-called comforters with their solid theology and tells them that if they were silent this would be closer to wisdom. The Psalms, the Wisdom literature, the book of Ecclesiastes and many more continually speak of the search for wisdom.

In Islam, truthfulness is arguably the most important of all the virtues required from a believer. The Qur'an records various categories of human beings of whom the Prophets are the highest and the most truthful ones next. Truthfulness is not just a matter of speaking truth – it includes the whole of the way a person lives their lives and relates both to behaviour and to internal mental states. Because of this, truthfulness is the cornerstone of an upright Muslim's character.

Ibn al-Qayyim, a leading Islamic scholar, said:

Truthfulness is the greatest of stations, from it sprout all the various stations of those traversing the path to God; and from it sprouts the upright path which if not trodden, perdition is that person's fate. Through it is the hypocrite distinguished from the believer and the inhabitant of Paradise from the

denizen of Hell. It is the sword of God in His earth: it is not placed on anything except that it cuts it; it does not face falsehood except that it hunts it and vanquishes it; whoever fights with it will not be defeated; and whoever speaks it, his word will be made supreme over his opponent. It is the very essence of deeds and the wellspring of spiritual states, it allows the person to embark boldly into dangerous situations, and it is the door through which one enters the presence of the One possessing Majesty. It is the foundation of the building of Islam, the central pillar of the edifice of certainty and the next level in ranking after the level of prophethood.
("The Virtue of Truthfulness", Madarij as-Salikeen)

The references of truthfulness in the Qur'an are constantly repeated:

O you who believe! Have fear of God, and be among the truthful. (Qu'ran 9:119)

And whosoever obeys God and His Messenger, such will be in the company of those whom God has blessed: the Prophets, the truthful ones, the martyrs, and the righteous. And how excellent a company are such people! (Qu'ran 4:69)

And mention in the Book, Abraham: surely he was a most truthful Prophet. (Qu'ran 19:41)

And mention in the Book, Ishmael: surely, he was a man true to his word, and he was a Messenger, a Prophet. (Qu'ran 19:54)

And mention in the Book, Enoch: surely he was a most truthful Prophet. (Qu'ran 19:56)

Joseph! O most truthful one! ... (Qu'ran 12:46)

The Messiah (Jesus), son of Mary, was no more than a Messenger; many were the Messengers that passed away before him. His mother (Mary) was a truthful one, a Believer... (Qu'ran 5:75)

Every major religion affirms the centrality of Truth. In the New Testament, people were amazed at the wisdom of Jesus. As a young child, Jesus is noted and is praised for his wisdom. God is described as wisdom itself and the source of all wisdom. Wisdom needs to be prayed for and is given by God. The Greek word for wisdom is 'sophia' and it is, perhaps, significant that it is regarded by many feminist writers today as a feminine rather than a masculine attribute.

It is not only in the West that religion has been hijacked. The same has happened in Hinduism, Buddhism and, most certainly, in Islam. In all too many parts of the Islamic world, particular texts from the Qur'an have been used to justify violence and suicide bombings. Intolerance and fundamentalism have been on the increase with the stress being placed on strict dress codes for women, sexual propriety and conforming to a fundamentalist understanding of Islamic doctrine and mores. The idea of Islam being about seeking the Eternal gets little attention. Yet here, as in other great religions, the reality that underpins Islam is still present. The Amman Declaration in 2007 represented a unanimous ruling by representatives of all the major branches of Islam which totally condemned violence and said:

Islam rejects extremism, radicalism and fanaticism – just as all noble, heavenly religions reject them – considering them as recalcitrant ways and forms of injustice. Furthermore, it is not a trait that characterizes a particular nation; it is an aberration that has been experienced by all nations, races, and religions. They are not particular to one people; truly they are a phenomenon that every people, every race and every religion has known.

We denounce and condemn extremism, radicalism and fanaticism today, just as our forefathers tirelessly denounced and opposed them throughout Islamic history. They are the ones who affirmed, as do we, the firm and unshakeable understanding that Islam is a religion of [noble] character traits in both its ends and means; a religion that strives for the good of the people, their happiness in this life and the next; and a religion that can only be defended in ways that are ethical; and the ends do not justify the means in this religion.

Too few Muslims take any notice of this extraordinary declaration coming from leaders of well over 95% of the world's Islamic groups, yet the Prophet Muhammad himself said, "My Ummah will not agree upon an error," so those fundamentalist Muslims who endorse violence, hatred and sectarianism are effectively calling the Prophet a liar. What is more, many ordinary Imams, local Muslims leaders, are unwilling to endorse the Amman Declaration and to speak out clearly to condemn the fundamentalist for fear of the power of the fundamentalists within their own congregations.

'Religion' has come to represent a distortion of the Eternal and, far from being a means to an end, it has become a sidetrack into which even the minority who profess interest in a broader vision of life are all too easily diverted. The illusion fosters the belief that the transcendent is only to be understood in religious categories and since these categories revolve round rituals, dogmas and belief systems, the voice of the Eternal is seldom heard. Kierkegaard says:

An illusion can never be destroyed directly, and only by indirect means can it gradually be removed... a direct attack only strengthens a person in his illusion. There is nothing that requires such gentle handling as an illusion, if one wishes to dispel it... That is what is achieved by the indirect method which... arranges everything dialectically for the prospective captive, and then shyly withdraws.

Indirect communication requires helping someone to 'see' something, bringing them to a realisation of a reality of which they may not previously have been aware. One does not communicate beauty or love by lecturing about it – all one can do is to help someone to begin on the inward journey to see the reality of these for themselves. If a child is brought up in a loveless household and, when they reach their teenage years, desperately seeks love with an inappropriate series of boyfriends or girlfriends only to find themselves 'dumped' after a few weeks or months, then the task of making the young adult aware that genuine love, commitment and self-sacrifice are possibilities is exceptionally difficult. The only way this can be achieved is through the individual coming to actually experience being loved. Since they are likely to reject this because their past experience has taught them to be cynical, this will not be easy.

An academic approach alone will never bring anyone to understand the existence of, still less the demand made by, the Eternal. This requires insight and an openness to an alternative perspective: A willingness to listen to the voice of the still small stream which endures in spite of the prancing of the dragons with which this book started. Most major religious writers have recognised this. St John of the Cross in his poem spoke of an understanding that goes beyond science:

This knowledge by unknowing
is such a soaring force
that scholars argue long
but never leave the ground.

Their knowledge always fails the source:
to understand unknowing,
rising beyond all science.
("I came into the unknown", St John of the Cross, 1542–1591)

Thomas Merton came to a sudden realization of a different way of looking at the world which saw all human beings united under an Eternal perspective which made everything else seem irrelevant. Pierre Teilhard de Chardin, SJ describes an awakening of a sense of just what it means to be human with all that means in terms of potentiality (*Le Sens Humain* or *The Sense of Man* in English translation, 1929). He also wrote of the growing indifference he found towards institutional Christianity which he described as "the sickness of Christianity". His insights have been amply confirmed since his death.

Institutional religion will largely collapse or fade into insignificance in the West as it is increasingly seen as irrelevant to the modern world, but beyond 'Religion' and beyond the 'post-truth' world lies the enduring values of the transcendent which will remain unchanged. The Eternal beckons gently and never forcefully. It calls in a still small voice but to hear this voice one needs to be open to the possibility of it being there. It will not be extinguished (hence the image of the stream with which this book started), and it represents in some ways the perennial philosophy that originated before Plato and which has constantly manifested itself in different forms around the world. People will never be brought to understand its importance by lectures, learned articles in academic journals or by direct communication – they need to be brought to 'see' something and this, as we have seen, involves indirect communication. It is partly an exercise in helping people to wake up and 'religion' rarely does this:

Spirituality means waking up. Most people, even though

they don't know it, are asleep. They're born asleep, they live asleep, they marry in their sleep, they breed children in their sleep, they die in their sleep without ever waking up. They never understand the loveliness and the beauty of this thing that we call human existence.

(Anthony de Mello, p. 5, quoted in Bernard Hoose's *Mysterious God*, 2014, p. 99)

Australia is a highly secular society and one of the few religious groups that are universally respected is the Salvation Army as they are always there for people when they are at their most desperate. When one has lost everything, been betrayed, loses one's job, is sleeping on the street and taking refuge in cheap drink and drugs then to suddenly discover that there are people who actually care and want to try and help without being judgmental can be genuinely transformative. This can be the beginning of an understanding that there is more to life than despair and hopelessness. The same can apply to the alcoholic or any other form of addition (including the addiction to the smart phone, appearance, success, money, sex or whatever other form of god is worshipped). If someone from the Salvation Army goes into the roughest and toughest Australian pub looking for support they will almost always find it as they are respected for the work they do. The same cannot be said for almost all other religious groups. A similar theme emerges in the Quaker tradition which has remained largely removed from dogmas and rituals and instead commits its members to living simply and standing for peace and justice as well as an attempt to seek the Eternal in stillness and silence. Yet, today, there are few Quakers.

The search for the Eternal is not a matter of assembling and assenting to complex theological theories – if it was it makes those who have doctorates in theology the closest to an understanding of what the Eternal means. Jesus did not come to proclaim theological doctrines. There is no direct mention in his teachings of ideas such as original sin, atonement, trinity, immaculate conception, salvation, papal infallibility and the like. These were later developments by Christian Church Fathers and others who were reflecting on the stories of the early Christians – and even these stories were selected from a large number of other texts in order to foster and affirm the reflections that the Church Fathers had arrived at. Jesus, by contrast, called people to follow him, to emulate him, to live the truth rather than know the truth. His true followers, he said, would be those who were committed to helping the poor, to visiting the sick and those in prison and to feeding the hungry. To live in this way is to commit oneself to living in the truth. This is precisely why Pilate's question, "What is truth?" was so radically misconceived. The irony is that the question was directed to Jesus who claimed to be truth, but not the truth as Pilate saw it. Pilate's question was reasonable; it is just the sort of question that any modern academic might ask and it was as unanswerable in Pilate's day as it is in ours. To ask the question in this way misses the point of Jesus' teaching which is to persuade those who wish to follow to stake everything on living out an apprehension of the Eternal in their daily lives. There is no certainty – only an existential commitment, born of insight, into something that transcends materialism and verificationism.

The same applies to the teachings of the Buddha, the prophet Muhammad, Guru Nanak and the great prophets and rabbis of Judaism as well as the Hindu Vedas. The Buddha's teaching as well as that of the great Hindu and Sikh sages were concerned with a change in the individual which involved great commitment and effort. They were all concerned with how life should be lived and with the transcendent dimension in life, but many of their subsequent followers have turned their teachings into doctrines and rituals. It is incredibly easy for means (rituals and dogmas) to become an end, and this is particularly so if the end that is desired is wisdom and an understanding about the

Eternal and the nature of human existence.

Václav Havel, poet, philosopher, playwright and former President of the Czech Republic, was imprisoned for four years by the Communist government. He was allowed to write one letter a week to his wife, Olga. On 7th January 1980 he wrote about a Prague greengrocer who ran a small shop. In the shop window he placed a sign saying, "Workers of the world unite." No one looking at the shop window took any notice of the sign – they had similar signs in their shops and offices, they were delivered every week by a government agency. The people looking in the shop window certainly noticed if there were any tomatoes, oranges or other fruit and whether they were fresh, but the sign was ignored. What, then, was the function of the sign? Havel says that it was put there by the greengrocer to say, "I will be a good communist. I will conform." Religion has become a matter of conformity which is why religious parents desire that their children conform to the same ideas and ways of behaving as they do. Conformity, however, will never bring anyone closer to an understanding of the radical nature of what an Eternal demand actually means.

There is a need to live in a world beyond God which nevertheless lives 'in God'. If this sounds a contradiction, it is not. Bonhoeffer was one of the first to recognise the need to die to the old idea of God. On 16th July 1944, he wrote to his friend (and later biographer) Eberhard Bethge saying: "We must live in the world as if there was no God – 'etsi deus non daretur' – God lets us know that we have to live as people who cope with life without God." Bonhoeffer was quoting Hugo Grotius, a 17th century theologian and lawyer who saw the Natural Law approach to ethics as not depending on the will of an omnipotent creator but on the structure of the universe and the nature of what it means to be human. Bishop John Robinson built on this idea in the 1960s in his book *Honest to God*. This is not an atheistic position – it is an affirmation of Eternal values built into the very structure of the universe, of love and creativity as an ultimate guiding principle underneath the whole of reality. It is this view of reality which is argued for by the great (albeit largely ignored) Jesuit theologian Roger Lenaers, SJ in his book *Living in God Without God* (Carysfort Press, 2017). He says:

> Today, when we use the traditional little word 'God', it should no longer refer to an almighty (and all good) reality outside the cosmos, capable of intervening in earthly events at will. It should refer to the spiritual fundamental reality which transcends all things and expresses itself in the form of the cosmos, makes itself visible, reveals itself, and does this by means of evolution. (p. 10)

A comparison, Lenaers argues, can be made with music. The genius of Mozart is given expression in sound waves but the sound waves alone cannot explain the genius which gives them life. The creativity of Mozart is a small reflection of the creativity of the cosmos (built in, as we have seen, in the potentiality latent in the singularity). Darwinian natural selection and verificationism see the universe as a result of chance driven by the forces of natural selection. Religion at its truest and best rejects this and sees the creativity of the Eternal underlying the whole of reality and giving birth, through its inbuilt creativity, to this reality. The universe is to be explained through the creativity and potentiality built into the very structures of reality.

Grace Jantzen argued for the world being seen as the body of God, Teilhard de Chardin saw God as the ground of our being. These, Lenaers and many others, are all pointing to the concept that the idea of God needs to be reconceptualized in the interests of Truth.

A common view today is that truth does not matter but love, pity and compassion do. The reverse is true. Truth is severe, harsh and demanding and it means facing up to the inadequacies of the old expressions of religion. Truth is the most fundamental thing of all. This was made clear in a dispute between two of the greatest influences on Hasidic Judaism – the Baal Shem Tov and the Kotzker.

The Baal Shem Tov inspired more Jews than, possibly, anyone else in history except the great Fathers of the Jewish faith. He had a hugely positive view of what it was to be human: Every human being was a dwelling place of God and God could be found in even the greatest sinner. The Baal Shem saw goodness everywhere and in everyone, and no one and nothing was separated from God's loving activity. The Jewish Temple had been the traditional centre of Jerusalem, but the Baal Shem established a new centre, the rabbi. Human beings, he maintained, could really be the dwelling place of God. God did not need an earthly temple, he dwelt in the hearts and minds of human beings.

Although the Baal Shem founded the Hasidic movement, his status was greater than that of the movement himself, such was his reputation that no one challenged him – except for one extraordinary but very different man – the Kotzker, Reb Menachem Mendl of Kotzk. Whereas the Baal Shem stressed love and compassion, the presence of God in every man and the goodness of all he saw, the Kotzker's position was very different, and in a way he opposed the Baal Shem by providing a different focus. The Kotzker stressed Truth whilst the Baal Shem stressed love and compassion and Abraham Joshua Heschel, in his book *A Passion for Truth*, makes clear the tension between the two.

The Baal Shem Tov's intention was to prevent Jewish piety from hardening into mere routine. Yet his path also became a habit, a routine. When first conceived, an idea is a break through, once adopted and repeated it becomes a cul de sac... Faith had become a way of life immune to challenge and doubt.

This is precisely what has happened when 'religion' becomes central. The Kotzker taught that Truth "could be reached only by way of the utmost freedom. Such freedom meant not to give in to any outside pressures, not to conform, not to please oneself or anyone else... He insisted that to get to the truth man had to go against himself and society. The true worship of God... was not in finding the Truth, but rather, in an honest search for it."

The Kotzker was in a direct line with the ancient Prophets of Israel preaching fury against the people – whereas the Baal Shem inspired joy, love and holiness, the Kotzker brought dread and contrition. For him, Truth was the absolute and the highest, and lack of integrity and lies were the opposite of Truth. Truth could not be felt where lies and deceit were present. Most people do not even care much for Truth and human beings will do almost anything to prevent it emerging as Truth is unsettling and uncomfortable, the very opposite of the secure life for which most people crave. People seek the comfort zone, they seek compromise and an accommodation with general opinion, which is why relativism and nihilism are so popular and whilst most people acquiesce with the idea of a post-truth world. The Kotzker contrasted to this the fearless commitment to truth.

Most religious thinkers have assumed that the predicament of man is due to his failure to obey the Law or to adhere to orthodox belief. Kierkegaard and the Kotzker saw its source in the ubiquitous pitfalls within the soul, in men's amazing disregard of their presence... Beware, they said, of too much faith, of blind belief in dogmas, of a willingness to weed out doubts rather than face them, for these speak of an unhealthy self-assurance precluding a reaching out for God. With incisive radicalism, the Kotzker set out to knock down the facades that thinkers have spent centuries constructing to protect man from the shattering recognition of the disparity between his desire for reward and contentment and religious demands for holiness and contrition...

The Kotzker insists that each individual has to make up their own mind about whether or not God exists. If there is no God then human beings are the measure of all things, but if there is a transcendent dimension, then it is Eternity that has the final measure. In the latter case there can be only one Truth and one standard for right and wrong. As Heschel puts it:

> What begins in a lie ends in blasphemy... Truth is often grey, and deceit is full of splendour. One must hunger fiercely after Truth to be able to cherish it... Truth is severe, harsh, demanding. We would rather hide our face in the sand than be confronted by it.

If someone asks what quality, without reservation, may be identified with the Divine, some would reply Love, or compassion or justice. The Kotzker maintained that it was Truth. Truth is not something that human beings can arrive at – it is an insight which must be striven for. As Heschel says:

> Mahatma Gandhi, one of the twentieth century's great seekers after justice, shared the insight of Kierkegaard and the Kotzker. On this point, he wrote, at the end of his autobiography, "My uniform experience has convinced me that there is no other God than Truth."

Opposition to this commitment to the absolute importance of Truth is easily explained. Most people want the comfort zone, they want moderation and the Aristotelian golden middle. The radical search for truth and integrity is too uncomfortable and people would prefer the security of belonging to a religious group or sect where they will be assured that all is well, that their group has the truth and all that is needed is conformity to the group. This is, however, precisely, a denial of the demand for personal integrity and the search for truth.

This passionate commitment to Truth and to the impact of truth on every aspect of life is held in common by the Kotzker, Kierkegaard, Wittgenstein and Havel. It is also affirmed in the Islamic tradition including by Jalaluddin Rumi:

> The truth was a mirror in the hands of God. It fell, and broke into pieces. Everybody took a piece of it, and they looked at it and thought they had the truth.

The following story is told about the Mullah Nasreddin. The Sultan of a great city was annoyed by the cheats and liars who entered his gates and caused trouble. He therefore set soldiers at all entrances. The soldiers were under orders to hang those who lied about their purpose for wishing to enter. Nasreddin saddled his donkey and rode to the city. At the gate, a guard stopped him and asked his purpose in wishing to enter and warned him that a lie would result in his being hanged. "This is good for I have come to be hanged," said Nasreddin. "You are a liar and will certainly hang!" said the guard. "Then you know I have spoken the truth and should not be hanged," said Nasreddin. Truth is certainly problematic but that does not mean it does not exist. All deep thinkers, for whom the problems of existence and life go to the very heart of who they are, recognised the centrality of Truth and all know how uncomfortable it is. All see Truth as very opposite of comfortable, 'cosy' religion. They were passionate about seeking truth and living truth but none ever claimed to have found it.

Lessing said:

> If God should hold enclosed in his right hand all truth, and in his left hand only the ever-active impulse after truth, although with the condition that I must always and forever err, I would

with humility turn to his left hand and say, "Father, give me this: pure Truth is for thee alone."

Every religion makes truth claims which it is impossible to verify and yet every religion shows a lack of humility about its own truth claims:

- Christians maintain that Jesus was born of a virgin, yet the Arians were incredibly influential and held that Jesus was the adopted son of God. This position was only refuted by the political power of two Roman emperors who opposed the Arians.
- Christians traditionally hold that God's Grace is necessary for someone to do good and original sin affects all human beings, but Pelagians held that any person can choose to do good or evil – yet Pelagians were eventually declared as heretics with little evidence to support their condemnation other than suppression by the (marginally) more powerful voices.
- Muslims claim that the Qur'an was literally dictated by God through the Archangel Gabriel and is meant to convey timeless truth, but to independent scholars all the evidence seems to point to the text being relative to the concerns the Prophet had when, respectively, in Mekka or Medina.
- Jews claim that God made a covenant promise with Abraham promising land in Palestine to Jews forever – yet many modern scholars doubt whether Abraham even existed and are convinced that the stories were written down hundreds of years after the events they purport to describe.

The lack of humility about doctrinal truth claims is found in every religion but this had much more to do with maintaining community cohesion and identity than any dispassionate search for ultimate Truth. Nevertheless, the fact that there is no neutral way of understanding objective truths like those above does not mean that adherents of each of these (and other) religions may not be living in relation to the Eternal. The various religions precisely express, in their different ways, affirmation of the transcendent and what it means.

Where is Truth? Not with those who assert they have it, but perhaps it is with those who do not know and try to live in relation to the Eternal, however they may define it. The old lady who goes to Mass each week; the aged Jewish homosexual who tries to live his commitment as he cares for his dying partner; the young unmarried Muslim woman who lives with her partner and who has lived with a number of others before and who takes her faith seriously and who struggles to try to live rightly before her God; the Sikh who regularly visits his mistress whilst still living with his wife but devotes his money and his life to the good of the weakest members of the community within which he lives; the abused woman who tries to stay faithful to her marriage vows whilst living with an abusive husband; the young man who tries to follow his God in uncertainty and ambiguity, wrestling with moral dilemmas and the challenges faced by a changing world, recognising goodness and truth in people from diverse culture and traditions as well as those who, whilst within his own tradition, take a completely different stance to his own may be closer to 'living in the truth' than those who claim to 'know the truth'. Truth is lived, it is not a matter of assent to doctrines.

The supposed 'heretics' who reject some of the dogmas of their own traditions but nevertheless seek the Eternal with passion, rejecting the preoccupation of their peers with social media, appearance and 'success' when all around them mock their search may be far closer to understanding the nature of the transcendent and the demands it makes than those who inhabit the often deadening routine of the 'religious' worlds.

Socrates found this, and the Oracle judged him the wisest man in Athens as a result. Truth is always an approximation. We may never have the whole story, but this does not mean that we may not have part of the story. Those who emphasise the importance of perspective are right and they are also right that for too long a patriarchal, rational, Western view of reality may have dominated and may have been seen as the only way of looking at truth. Isaac Newton said:

> I do not know what I may appear to the world, but to myself I seem to have been only like a boy playing on the sea-shore, and diverting myself in now and then finding a smoother pebble or a prettier shell than ordinary, whilst the great ocean of truth lay all undiscovered before me.

Those who affirm the Eternal claim that science can only take us so far and that there is a broader dimension to reality. What matters is not knowing the truth but living in the Truth – being willing to stake one's life on transcendent values and to live a life of integrity and commitment to the Absolute that the Eternal represents. Whether or not there is a life after death is a secondary issue: If there is, then no one who commits their life to the Eternal has anything to fear. If there is no survival of death then there is no better or more fulfilling life than to live one's life in this way and to die peacefully knowing that one has done so. A post-truth existence, by contrast, leads only to despair and disillusionment at the futility and meaninglessness of existence. Those advocating its adoption are concerned with power and the destruction of any idea of meaning or value. As such, they need to be resolutely opposed.

Wherever Truth is, therefore, it is least likely to be found amongst religious fundamentalists and they are best avoided or approached with the greatest of caution. By contrast, those people who wrestle with ambiguity, for whom much is unclear, who have a broad commitment to the common human search for understanding and meaning, those who are willing to learn from others and accept that whatever their position, they could be wrong, such people have precisely the marks of those who are seeing a realistic understanding of truth. This is not an accident, it is a necessary consequence of the Truth claims they are espousing.

Affirmation of a transcendent dimension to reality, to the creativity, love and values underpinning the cosmos, to the ideas of meaning and hope in the face of despair are central to religion – and it is to this that traditional talk of 'god' should point. 'Religion' has, however, largely lost sight of what is essential and, because of this, will decline into irrelevance unless an unlikely transformation takes place.

Chapter Eleven

The Relevance of the Eternal

Instead of the rise of AI we are looking at the fall of human beings. The majority of people no longer aspire to greatness since all supposedly great people are regarded as radically flawed and the media seek to show their weakness and to demonstrate how fallible, how 'human', how like us they really are. At the most people may aspire to success which is measured in financial or reputational terms. Even the most admirable figures are seen to be weak and flawed; they have sexual, financial or character faults. Everyone is damaged and diminished. Tall poppies must be cut down to size. People no longer aspire to wisdom since, in a post-truth world, wisdom does not exist. Beauty no longer makes a demand on us since beauty is culturally relative and depends on media exposure. Love is ephemeral and instead of entering into committed, long-term relationships we recognise that relationships and loves are transitory. Everything passes. We are afloat in a sea of flux and occasionally ask ourselves, "Is this it?" before distracting ourselves with work, shopping, our smart phone or a new relationship.

We no longer educate our children. The word 'education' comes from the Latin 'educare' which means to 'bring out' to help them on a journey to fulfil their potential. However, since most people deride the idea of human potential, the only aim is to educate people to be economically effective units, to prepare them for the workplace so that they can strive to pay the mortgage, struggle to raise their children on wages or salaries that are all too often declining in real terms and eventually retire, play golf, cultivate the garden and die. We are like bees conditioning our young for particular tasks to serve the hive that is modern urban civilisation. No one any longer asks to what end we strive, since talk of ends or purposes is now passé, out of date and irrelevant. Meaning is constructed in the here and now by media as well as our obsession with sport, shopping, appearance and fame. We have created new and intangible gods and we continuously bow down and worship at their altars.

We have lost our sense of wonder, of the infinite possibility of being human. Joy is extinguished and instead we aspire to 'happiness' without really considering what this means. With the death of Truth comes the death of a broader vision of being human. We are educating our children to be advanced AI and in so doing have lost sight of essential human capacities and potentialities. Education is preoccupied with 'facts' and accumulating knowledge – most of which the young person will never use. It focuses on STEM subjects (particularly science and mathematics) and neglects what it means to be human. We have conquered the world and think we have understood it and have ended up impoverished and diminished. We have, like Jacob, sold our birthright for a mess of porridge. We have failed our children by not providing them with the tools to think critically and deeply, and to ponder the most important questions in life.

Teaching used to be a high, respected and noble calling. People entered the profession because they cared about young people entrusted to them and saw their task as being to help them fulfil their potential not just academically but in sport, music and, above all, in developing their potential as human beings. Increasingly, however, teachers are monitored and measured to ensure that they achieve 'results' which translate into academic results. The result is that the original vision which led many to become teachers has been ground down to something debased.

The potentiality of the human spirit has been eroded and our children suffer. Pornography, the Internet and the constant attention of the smart phone have led us away from what we are meant to be. Religion is widely derided among the young, and declining numbers in Churches in the Western world are mostly drawn from the retired. Where there is growth in religion it is usually grounded on one or more forms of fundamentalism. Social justice, the demands for compassion, empathy, care for the vulnerable, the immigrant and the refugee are widely disparaged. Even the most prestigious charities have representatives that are flawed and sometimes exploit those they are meant to help. Old people are packed into 'care' homes and the Japanese and others are looking for ways to have them entertained and 'looked after' by advanced AI which can play games with them, talk to them, feed them and clean them – what more, it is argued, is there to life? We are too busy to care for or respect the old, so we delegate and dehumanise. The same applies at the other end of life.

At the end of the 19th century, life was very hard for most people but one person (usually the man) could work and another could care for, love and look after children. In the 1950s and 1960s women could find employment if they wished but if they preferred to stay at home with the children this was economically possible – they had the possibility of making a choice. Today, however, two people have to work to keep a family with a roof over their heads, food on the table and warmth during long winter nights. 'Family time' barely exists as the pressure of daily life and the attractions of social media atomize families and undermine community. More and more are vulnerable and survival, even in the West, becomes a real issue – yet hardly anyone cares. The English film *I, Daniel Blake* (winner of the Palme d'Or at the Cannes Film Festival) is all too searingly real with its portrayal of the poor and their vulnerability. In the United States it is even worse with tens of millions living in poverty and without hope. They are told they are free and that they live in 'the land of the free' but everywhere they are in chains. They are wage slaves compelled, in tens of millions of cases, to work without hope in order to survive. Most of us do not want to confront the reality of quiet desperation that the lives of millions of people represent as it makes us feel too uncomfortable.

In short, we have lost our way or, to put it more briefly, we are lost. We have conquered the world but lost whatever the word 'soul' once stood for. Religion is no longer much help as it has become a largely empty vessel which no longer conveys any real idea of meaning, of truth or of a different way of living life. Instead of being a means to an end, 'religion' has become an end in itself and, by so doing, has lost its vigour and relevance. It is increasingly a mark of identity and community belonging, and even this is being displaced by new identities formed by supporting particular sports teams, political parties or identifying online with a community of like-minded persons. In the US, identity is increasingly found through the party ticket one voted for in the last election and the population is becoming increasingly polarized. Media outlets support this polarization and make it hard to understand a broader perspective. The US media in particular takes a US view of the world and most people have no interest in the lives or prospects of those in sub-Saharan Africa, in Afghanistan, Pakistan, Yemen or Venezuela.

And yet, in spite of everything, the spirit of real humanity refuses to die or to be totally silenced. In the Hebrew Scriptures, the book of Ecclesiastes says (3:11):

> He has made everything appropriate in its time. He has also set eternity in the heart of human beings, yet so that they will not find out the work which God has done from the beginning even to the end.

In a way, death is the key – it confronts everyone who is willing to think about it with the transitory nature of human existence. Plato said those who really study philosophy properly are preparing themselves for death. The whole of the Harry Potter books are about death. For Voldemort, death is the ultimate evil which he will do everything to avoid including killing and creating Horcruxes. He says, "There is no good or evil, only power and those with the will to use it." By contrast Dumbledore, Sirius and others see in death the beginning of a new adventure.

Steve Jobs, the founder and for many years the genius behind Apple Computers, in an address to students at Stanford University in 2005 said:

> When I was 17 I read a quote that went: If you live each day as if it was your last, some day you'll most certainly be right. I have looked in the mirror every morning and asked myself: "If today were the last day of my life, would I want to do what I am about to do today?" and whenever the answer has been NO for too many days in a row, I know I need to change something. Remembering that I'll be dead soon is the most important tool I've ever encountered to help me make the big choices in life. Because almost everything – all external expectations, all pride, all fear of embarrassment or failure – these things just fall away in the face of death, leaving only what is truly important. Remembering that you are going to die is the best way I know to avoid the trap of thinking you have something to lose. You are already naked. There is no reason not to follow your heart.

And then he goes on to say, "About a year ago I was diagnosed with cancer…"

> No one wants to die. Even people who want to go to heaven don't want to die to get there. And yet death is the destination we all share. No one has ever escaped it. And that is as it should be, because death is very likely the single best invention of life. It is life's change agent. It clears out the old to make way for the new. Right now the new is you, but someday not too long from now, you will gradually become the old and be cleared away. Sorry to be so dramatic, but it is quite true. Your time is limited, so don't waste it living

someone else's life. Don't be trapped by dogma – which is living with the results of other people's thinking. Don't let the noise of others' opinions drown out your own inner voice. And, most important, have the courage to follow your heart and intuition. They already know what you truly want to become. Everything else is secondary.

The weakness of Jobs' claim is that everyone does not know what they want to become since they have been deprived of the opportunity by the forces of culture and lack of real education. One of the greatest choices facing any human being is one that few even consider – and that is whether we are, indeed, simply animals who are born, grow, reproduce and die whilst creating some form of imagined meaning for ourselves whilst we distract ourselves to avoid the meaninglessness of existence or facing the existential challenge of realising that there is something more. This is what traditional talk of an Eternal dimension to life is meant to convey – it points to a different way of looking at the world and assessing meaning and purpose. It is this that Plato sought to show his students (cf. p. 17), it is what Clifford talks about when using the parable of the Trilobites (p. 126), and it has been the essence of the perspective for which all major religions have stood – before they became institutionalized.

Where is the transcendent to be found in the modern world? There are two ways of approaching this question and it depends on asking, 'What is Eternity', and what does reference to 'The Eternal' stand for? 'The Eternal' may refer to:

1. A state of being after death. This is the most common view – that eternity is a state of post-mortem existence which will either:
   a) Continue forever in some type of temporal paradise which is often portrayed as a state that brings maximal happiness. This is usually defined in terms that the

society of the time recognises as being a maximally happy state. For the Norse warriors it was a constant banquet in Valhalla with other great warriors enjoying feasting and copious quantities of ale; for Christians it is often portrayed as a kingdom of peace and love ruled over by the risen Lord Jesus, and for Muslims it is a somewhat hedonistic paradise with young girls and boys attending to every need of the faithful accompanied by cool water and wonderful fruits (which would be desirable to a people whose ideas developed in the deserts of Arabia).

b) For Catholics, drawing on previous Islamic philosophers as well as on Aristotle, it is the timeless beatific vision of God. Since God in mainstream Catholic theology (following St Thomas Aquinas, St Augustine, Maimonides and the early Islamic philosophers) is timeless, spaceless, bodiless and wholly simple, so the faithful will become timeless and 'see God'.

In all cultures this post-mortem existence (for those who believe in it) is seen as a state of being where suffering comes to an end and where joy is unsurpassed.

Such a state after death may or may not exist – there is no clear evidence either way and the question of life after death remains an open one. There can be legitimate views on both sides of the debate as to the plausibility of post-mortem existence and which of the varied accounts, if any, is regarded as the most persuasive, but there is no proof or even convincing evidence one way or another.

2. The second possibility is rather different and is more important. It refers to a different way of living in the here and now. To 'live in the Eternal' is to live one's life in a different way. Henry David Thoreau put it well:

If a man does not keep pace with his companions, perhaps

it is because he hears a different drummer. Let him step to the music which he hears, however measured or far away.

Living in the eternal means accepting an absolute set of values grounded in the centrality of Wisdom, Beauty, Creativity, Compassion, Mercy, Forgiveness, Forbearance, Patience, Inner Strength and Humility. It is to live according to the great virtues that have been affirmed throughout human history and to be willing to stake one's life on the possibility that it is in so doing that true human fulfilment is to be found. It is to affirm that human beings have a common potential and fulfilling this potential is the only way of achieving real happiness because it is grounded in the human nature all human beings share. This is a rejection of relativism, and an affirmation that every human being is called to fulfil their potential by living according to Eternal values.

There are considerable philosophic difficulties with the idea of life after death. As explained on page 163, there are, essentially, three possibilities which relate to different ways of understandings what it means to be human.

1. Dualism holds that human beings are made up of two irreducible substances – soul and body.
2. Material Monism maintains that human beings are made up simply of matter and that every aspect of being human including love, the idea of freedom, beauty and consciousness can be explained in material terms.
3. The third possibility is Monist idealism which holds that there is only a single reality (hence 'monism') but instead of the reality being matter it is mind or consciousness. Matter, in this view, depends on consciousness not the

other way round.

None of these explanations are satisfactory and if there is a life after death it must be accepted that we have little idea of what form it would take or, indeed, whether it is possible. This is not surprising as if there is survival then it is certain to be radically different from anything we can understand this side of the grave. However, perhaps this is not the central issue. Whilst most people identify talk of 'Eternity' with life after death, since there is no compelling evidence for this one way or another the question of life after death must remain open. Christians maintain that Jesus rose from the dead, but the claim is a faith claim which may or may not be true – in precisely that same way that the claim that God dictated the Qur'an to the Prophet Muhammad may or may not be true, or the claim in Judaism that God promised a certain land to Abraham and his descendants. Within Christianity, Islam and Judaism these claims are held with passion and intensity but for anyone standing outside these frameworks the question must remain an open one. If the only motive for living one's life according to a set of enduring values is the hope of some form of immortal existence, then this is a morally debased approach: It is akin to the child bribed by sweets or the reluctant SS guard going along with his assignment to Auschwitz because of the hope of promotion. To speak of the Eternal as representing a different way of living life in response to a transcendent dimension to the universe is a different matter and a claim of a different order. It does not depend on any hope of a reward.

In a post-truth, post-modern, nihilistic world, the idea of 'Eternal values' will be derided but these values have endured throughout history in spite of many attempts to destroy them or to render them meaningless. They are mocked by the materialists who see the world as devoid of meaning or purpose but it is precisely meaning and purpose that these Eternal values affirm. There is no proof that such eternal values exist which is why abductive arguments are the only ones that will have any validity. These seek (as set out on p. 118) to provide the most persuasive account of all the evidence available whilst accepting that other explanations are perfectly possible and could be right. Søren Kierkegaard recognised this when he said that faith means staking one's life on something whilst recognising that the possibility of error always exists. Faith is full of ambiguity and uncertainty but that does not invalidate it – indeed fundamentalists and their certainties are dangerous in any area and nowhere more so than in dealing with the Eternal. Humility is essential and is part of being human. Dietrich Bonhoeffer recognised this when he agonized over taking part in a plot to assassinate Hitler. He was a convinced and dedicated pacifist yet seeing the enormous suffering that the Nazi party caused and having seen the effect of their policies he felt called to act whilst knowing that what he was doing could still be wrong.

Søren Aabye Kierkegaard lived in a Denmark dominated in intellectual circles by the philosophy of Hegel. Hegel's philosophy was, in its turn, to lead to Marx and to the rejection of God. Hegel had gone a long way down this path – for Hegel 'Geist', or Absolute Spirit, was not an existing reality, ontologically independent of the Universe and on which the Universe depended. Instead Geist was emerging into consciousness through human reason. The German nation and the German intellectual tradition represented, for Hegel, the pinnacle of human achievement and the most advanced stage of the development towards Geist or the Absolute Idea. Geist emerged through history (and Hegel was the first to write a philosophy of history) through the operation of the Dialectical process whereby one view was put forward representing a thesis, a counter view was proposed presenting an antithesis, and out of the tension between these two positions a new and higher level insight emerges which forms a synthesis. This, in turn, becomes a new thesis which will be opposed by a new antithesis and this will give rise to a new synthesis and so the process continues throughout history.

For Hegel, religious claims such as those made by Christianity were to a certain extent true – but certainly not absolutely true. They represented a stage in the gradual emergence of the Absolute Idea and, for Hegel, Philosophy was supreme about theology. Kierkegaard rejected Hegel's whole approach root and branch. He considered it to be naïve and foolish in the extreme. He was a philosophic realist in the classic tradition. Whereas Hegel is sometimes nicknamed 'Both/And' because of the importance he attaches to the dialectical process, Kierkegaard was named 'Either/Or'. Either God exists or God does not. Either Jesus was God Incarnate or he was not. Either death is the end of human existence or it is not. Kierkegaard allows no ambiguity – there is a truth at stake and this truth cannot be compromised. There is here a clash in understandings of truth. Hegel was to provide the seeds which led indirectly to the death of truth whereas Kierkegaard affirms the centrality of absolute truth.

Kierkegaard affirms bivalence and in so doing challenges the whole post-modern, anti-realist, perspectival approach to truth. He is quite prepared to accept that there may be no Absolute, no Eternal dimension and no meaning to life but what he will argue for, passionately, is that there is a truth to be affirmed, or rejected. For Kierkegaard, the temporal realm can only lead to despair. Kierkegaard considered that a human being could only become that of which he or she was capable (in other words they could only fulfil their human potential) in response to and in relationship with the transcendent. Human potentiality, therefore, is grounded in a relation to what some might call Absolute or the Eternal. The human call was to live in relationship with this reality, a relationship which should be at the centre of an individual's life and which could, in extreme cases such as that of Abraham, call people beyond the demands of the conventional ethics of contemporary society. Only living in this way could provide the path to truth and to overcoming meaninglessness and despair.

Kierkegaard, unlike almost any other theologian or philosopher, refuses to do theology in the sense of talking about God. God, for Kierkegaard, was 'the Unknown' and he refused to speculate about the nature of this reality. Surprisingly this is not dissimilar to St Thomas Aquinas although Aquinas, unlike Kierkegaard, thought that God's existence could be proved whereas Kierkegaard maintained that such an attempt was absurd. At the most any proof, even if it succeeded, could show that God existed but this would not be enough to engender the absolute existential faith response that true belief represented. For Teilhard de Chardin, God was "the ground of our being", that which is most fundamental in the universe, that which underpins all reality. For Karl Rahner, SJ God was "Holy Mystery". It is precisely to this ultimate reality, this ground of our being, the ultimate Mystery to which talk of the Eternal points.

Kierkegaard, therefore, thought that faith represented an unproved and unprovable assumption that there exists The Unknown or the transcendent, which some term God, and that living in the truth means living in relationship to this reality. He rejects the attempt to arrive at truth objectively as any such attempt will only be an approximation and will never provide sufficient certainty to be the basis for staking one's life. Faith precisely involves subjectivity as it means an inner appropriation of a commitment to a relationship. In a way it is like love – being able to talk about one's beloved is not the same as loving him or her. Kierkegaard concentrates on what it means for an individual to live in relationship with the Absolute. The 'how' of the way one lives can give the 'what' of the Absolute or the Eternal, but concentration on the objective facts yields nothing except objective facts, and certainly does not yield faith which depends on a subjective acceptance of objective truths. Kierkegaard is a realist who clearly recognises that faith is not about simple assent to realist truth claims. It is about the transformation of a human life in response to these claims.

Kierkegaard wished to move people away from the usual, objective way of talking about truth. He quotes the epistle of James:

You believe in God? You do well. The Devils also believe and tremble.

In other words the devils believe THAT God exists, they do not 'believe in' or centre their lives on God. Someone may believe that the world is round because they have been told this is the case and have seen photographs, but Christopher Columbus believed in the world being round and staked his life on it when he attempted to sail round a world which others considered to be flat. It is this that makes religious truth subjective – and it is this that has given rise to so much misunderstanding of Kierkegaard's thought.

In *Concluding Unscientific Postscript*, Kierkegaard (through his pseudonym Johannes Climacus) claims that "truth is subjectivity" and this is a misleading expression which has led to much confusion. Various questions in life can be looked at either objectively or subjectively – for instance what it means to get married, what it means to die or what it means to pray. Objectively the first of these might involve consideration of the marriage service, the formalities involved, the legal implications, whether a marriage can be dissolved and perhaps the cost as well as similar practical issues. When, however, the question of marriage is raised subjectively then it is a different matter – it becomes necessary to consider existential questions such as 'what does it mean for me to get married', 'what is the significance of marriage for my life'. In a similar fashion, discussion of the eternal objectively can be the subject of academic papers and discussion of the evidence in favour or against. It can also raise questions whether a human person survives death, whether the soul alone survives or whether there is a new body, whether one retains one's memories and so on. Such objective questions leave out the passionate interest of the individual in these issues and Kierkegaard considered that the really important issues were raised when these questions were addressed subjectively. For instance, what does it mean for me and the way I live my life that I shall survive death? What effect will this have on all my actions and how will my life be transformed? What is the significance for me that there can be a transcendent element in human beings as well as Eternal values? These are questions of a different order to objective questions. Columbus' whole life was affected by his belief that the world was round and Kierkegaard's point is that faith in the eternal should have a similar, subjective impact.

People who are considered to be wise may accumulate much objective knowledge, but this knowledge is not existentially significant. Kierkegaard puts it this way:

> ... what is most difficult of all for the wise man to understand is precisely the simple. The plain man understands the simple directly, but when the wise man sets himself to understand it, it becomes infinitely difficult... the more the wise man thinks about the simple... the more difficult it becomes for him.
> (*Concluding Unscientific Postscript* [*CUP*], p. 160, Princeton University Press)

Kierkegaard's complaint is against philosophers, theologians and others who busy themselves building up more and more learning and lose touch with the simple. In particular they lose touch with the essential nature of faith and its impact on the lives of individuals. A person can become so stuffed with theological or philosophical knowledge that he or she never gets round to living the simple life of faith. Human beings busy themselves with worldly, temporal tasks and so lose interest in the real issue of how to live. Questions such as 'How should I live?' or 'What does it mean for me to have faith?' can mistakenly seem, with much learning, to become irrelevant. Such vital questions concern young and older people and have traditionally been at the very heart of philosophical reflection, yet are today considered naïve and unworthy of debate by academic philosophers and theologians. Indeed today's philosophers rarely comment on any of the central issues of our day and this is a reflection of the way in which the discipline has largely become irrelevant to the lives of most people. Kierkegaard thinks that most philosophers are good talkers and writers but fail to express anything significant with their lives. As he says:

> The police thoroughly frisk suspicious persons. If the mobs of speakers, teachers, professors, etc., were to be thoroughly frisked in the same way, it would no doubt become a complicated criminal affair. To give them a thorough frisking – yes, to strip them of the clothing, the changes of clothing... to frisk them by ordering them to be silent, saying: Shut up, and let us see what your life expresses, for once let this be the speaker who says what you are.
> (*Søren Kierkegaard's Journals and Papers*, Hong & Hong, 3:2334)

Instead of living in a world of words that have ceased to have any impact, philosophers, theologians and teachers should be judged by how they live. An individual's life is the best expression of what he or she believes – not the words that are said or the institutions of which they consider themselves to be members. Indeed Kierkegaard wishes to bring people to be silent, to cease to take refuge in language and instead to consider who they are before the Eternal. Kierkegaard says:

> When the question of truth is raised in an objective manner, reflection is directed objectively to the truth, as an object to

which the knower is related. Reflection is not focused upon
the relationship, however, but upon the question of whether
it is the truth to which the knower is related... Let us take as
an example the knowledge of God. Objectively, reflection is
directed to the problem of whether this object is the true God;
subjectively, reflection is directed to the question whether the
individual is related to something in such a manner that his
relationship is in truth a God relationship. (*CUP*, p. 178)

'Truth is subjectivity' is an ambiguous phrase. It is often taken to
mean that whatever someone believes in becomes true for them.
This was Sartre's understanding and led to the importance he
attached to personal authenticity and to the whole movement
of existentialism which calls individuals to say an emphatic
'yes' to a meaningless universe and to live passionately in the
light of this knowledge. This is not Kierkegaard's meaning. He
maintains the realist position that:

1. Either there are Eternal values and a transcendent order
   on which the Universe depends,
2. Or there are not.

This issue cannot be settled by rational proof. The existence of
Eternal values cannot be known to be true or false but there
is nevertheless a truth at stake. Kierkegaard is an ontological
realist but epistemologically he accepts that human beings have
no guaranteed access to the truth. This does not mean, however,
that they can be indifferent to it – instead they have to stake their
lives on a claim to truth even though this may not be capable
of proof. Faith in a transcendent order requires a passion and
commitment that staking one's life necessarily involves, but it
is also accompanied by the knowledge that one could be wrong.
No one can do any more than staking one's life but religious faith
requires nothing less. Religious faith means being suspended

over 70,000 fathoms, risking one's life on a claim to truth that may be false and that cannot be proved:

> The wader feels his way with his foot lest he gets beyond his depth; and so the shrewd and prudent man feels his way with the understanding in the realm of the probable and finds God where the probabilities are favourable and gives thanks when he has acquired a good livelihood and there is probability besides for early advancement; when he has found himself a pretty and attractive wife... of the type of beauty that will last a long time, and that her physique is such that she will in all probability give birth to strong and healthy children. To believe against the understanding is something different and to believe with the understanding cannot be done at all. (*CUP*, p. 232)

Faith involves a total commitment which is nevertheless possibly false. This is part of being a realist, to admit that one can be wrong. This is why abductive arguments which seek to arrive at the most persuasive explanation are the only ones that are relevant. Once this is understood, it should necessarily lead to humility. It is one thing to stake one's own life with passion and total commitment on a set of beliefs, but once one has seen that what one is staking one's life on could in principle be false, one has no right to impose one's beliefs and commitments on others – yet it is precisely this that many of those who claim to know the truth persist in doing and their position rests on confusion. This applies not least in Islam today but in many other religions and cultures as well.

The position is well expressed in CS Lewis' children's story called *The Silver Chair*. In this story there is a character called Puddleglum, a Marsh-wiggle, who is a permanent pessimist, always expecting disaster. He is accompanied by two children, and they are searching for a lost Prince. They become trapped in an underground world by an evil witch. Just as they are making plans to leave the underground kingdom (having found the Prince) the witch, the Lady of the Green Kirtle, walks in and stops their escape. Rather than using force, the Lady, with the help of a fragrant fire and magic, tries to convince Puddleglum and company that neither Narnia nor Aslan nor anything in the world above ground ('Overland' representing the Eternal) is real and therefore they have no reason to leave. The witch uses her powers to try to persuade her captives to forget the world above, telling them that their idea of a sun simply stems from seeing lamps and wishing for a bigger better lamp, and their idea of a lion (in the story Aslan the great lion is intended to represent Jesus – Lewis is a Christian writer) stems from seeing cats and wishing for a bigger and better cat (there are echoes here of Freud). The witch's arguments are persuasive and seem to account for the facts as they are experienced by the small party. There are parallels here with Plato's story of being imprisoned in a cave or with the idea of a transcendent world held to by most major religions.

It is a fascinating scene that culminates with an inspiring speech from the least likely of heroes: Puddleglum. After a few moments, he answers the witch:

"One word, Ma'am," he said... "One word. All you've been saying is quite right, I shouldn't wonder. I'm a chap who always liked to know the worst and then put the best face I can on it. So I won't deny any of what you said. But there's one thing more to be said, even so. Suppose we have only dreamed, or made up, all those things – trees and grass and sun and moon and stars and Aslan himself. Suppose we have. Then all I can say is that, in that case, the made-up things seem a good deal more important than the real ones. Suppose this black pit of a kingdom of yours is the only world. Well, it strikes me as a pretty poor one. And that's a funny thing, when you come to think of it. We're just babies making up a game, if you're right. But four babies playing a game can make a play-world which licks your real world hollow. That's why I'm going to stand by the play-world. I'm on Aslan's side even if there isn't any Aslan to lead it. I'm going to live as like a Narnian as I can even if there isn't any Narnia. So, thanking you kindly for our supper, if these two gentlemen and the young lady are ready, we're leaving your court at once and setting out in the dark to spend our lives looking for Overland. Not that our lives will be very long, I should think; but that's small loss if the world's as dull a place as you say." (CS Lewis, *The Silver Chair*)

Puddleglum doesn't waste a lot of time and energy debating with the Lady of the Green Kirtle. In fact, he actually concedes that what she is saying may really be true. Lewis uses his writings to challenge contemporary understandings of the truth and to show that what matters is action.

For Puddleglum, truth isn't found in intellectual debate, but in living a particular way of life. It is about living according to transcendent values and staking one's life on the claim that these exist and are real. Søren Kierkegaard made the same point when he said, "As you have lived, so have you believed." Standing for the truth requires living in the truth and this requires a radical commitment to the poor, the weak, the marginalised and those unable to care for themselves. It requires sacrificing one's own interests for a wider vision. It demands marching to a different drummer than that accepted by modern culture and most contemporaries.

One can, of course, stand on the fence. One can be an agnostic and say, "I do not know whether or not there are Eternal values and until this can be proved I will do nothing." This, however, is in itself to make a choice, it is to make a decision. One is committed to life, there is no choice but to decide.

Once to every man and nation,
comes the moment to decide,
In the strife twixt truth and falsehood
For the good or evil side.
(James Russell Lowell, 1884)

It is not, however, about a once and for all decision, but about committing one's life to living in accordance with transcendent values or to rejecting these. Every moment of every day reinforces the choice because it is how one conducts one's life that determines what one regards as true. Indifference and agnosticism are not options.

Complaining about the state of the world and how terrible and unjust it appears to be is all very well but it contains an element of self-indulgence. The real test is what one will do in response. 'It is better to light a candle than to curse the darkness' and lighting a candle requires not words but action. The issue is engagement rather than apathy; action rather than lassitude; hope rather than despair. Engagement involves politics, business, the arts and every aspect of life. To speak of the Eternal is not to advocate an escape with the world but precisely a full engagement with it – albeit an engagement that recognises the importance of transcendent values which are worth standing for and, if necessary, dying for since it is only these values that endure.

Escaping from the pain and apparent futility of the universe through drugs, drink, shopping or social media are rational responses. If the universe and life are, indeed, meaningless; if nature is "red in tooth and claw"; if human beings are simply animals that have evolved by natural selection without meaning except for reproductive success; if there is no hope except an end to suffering and failure then escaping from these makes a degree of sense. In *Studies in Pessimism* Schopenhauer examined suicide as a response to pain and meaninglessness, and rejected the idea that it was morally wrong. The only valid argument against suicide, he claimed, was that in attempting to escape meaninglessness it offers an apparent rather than a real good as if, as religious people tend to maintain, it is through suffering that the highest values can be achieved then suicide negates this possibility. Seneca and Pliny both approved of suicide, Aristotle did not condemn it on moral grounds although he did on social grounds. David Hume in *On Suicide* which was published after his death argued for it as an escape from meaninglessness and adversity. The necessity that seems inevitably to lead to utter depression and total despair provokes suicide as an apparently rational choice. It is an understandable reaction.

The argument against this should not be based on morality but on the state of the universe. If there are, indeed, Eternal values (and there may not be) then there is something worth living and fighting for whatever one's own existential state. There is also the possibility of hope in the midst of what seems utter hopelessness – that on the other side of total despair new possibilities may be open. It is here, possibly, that the only antidote to despair may be found – in the seemingly remote possibility of hope in spite of all the evidence. Bonhoeffer was a shining example when he, in the degradation of a concentration camp, continued to inspire inmates with a sense of hope and purpose before going to his own death.

In the 1929 Wall Street crash, some people committed suicide because of the loss of all their money; some people took the same route because they have been betrayed in a relationship; others have done so because their reputation was destroyed or because a life that seemed full of promise has turned into a blind alley which apparently leads nowhere. However real and terrible these and other scenarios are, the claim that there are transcendent values carries with it the possibility of hope despite despair, of possibility rather than the grip of necessity, of a new start even though this seems impossible.

One of the most important religious teachings is the possibility of forgiveness, a new beginning and hope no matter what the external circumstances. The very idea seems almost impossible to accept – the claim that whatever one has done, whatever one's offence against the established order a new start may be open and that, even in utter degradation and failure, there is still hope is very hard to accept when one is in the grip of a post-truth world. The person in despair will laugh in derision at these possibilities. They would see the necessity of failure and desolation with all that goes with these states as being inevitable and inescapable. Talk of Eternal values and of hope in the face of apparent meaninglessness and despair rejects this inevitability.

Chapter Twelve

Where is the Eternal to be Found?

Amicus Plato, amicus Aristoteles, magis amica veritas.
Isaac Newton
(Plato is my friend, Aristotle is my friend, but my greatest friend is truth.)

A culture of narcissism has gained a strong foothold in much of the Western world. The emphasis is on 'me' and 'my' needs – a culture of my selfie, my needs, my profile, and 'because I'm worth it' has led to many governments, including that of the United States, being in the hands of narcissistic personalities. The anonymity of cyberspace has facilitated violence, bullying, and frighteningly explicit pornography which is available to children at a younger and younger age.

The search for truth and moral rules in isolation from life can be regarded as a function of legal or academic studies of ethics and becomes a somewhat arid, masculine enterprise which tries to tie down both religion and morality into firm categories. Wisdom and relationships, by contrast, require a more wholistic approach. The story is told of a man who could take a flower and pluck every part of it naming every one, but what he could not see was the beauty of the flower. Many modern philosophers (particularly in the United States, the United Kingdom and Australia) behave in the same way – they dissect language and life into such narrow categories that they lose sight of wisdom. In practice, this applies to a great deal of philosophy as it is practised in the modern academic world. Sophia requires a broader perspective than the narrow, analytic approach to philosophy which has for too long dominated Western thought.

A search for wisdom involves a change in oneself. Only

the wise person can be wise whilst a foolish person may know something true. The wise person is not the same as the clever or the intelligent person, nor the same as the person who knows many 'truths'. A philosopher should be someone who knows nothing and is troubled to the depths of her being by her ignorance. Too few modern, professional philosophers are disturbed and troubled in this way. Wise people are generally humble – they are the reverse of arrogant. Wittgenstein had a great admiration for those metaphysicians of the past who struggled to find a way of understanding knowledge and reality. These individuals showed passion and commitment to the search which they pursued with integrity and with every fibre of their being. By contrast, many modern philosophers are merely clever.

Living by Eternal values means, above all else, a life of integrity and this is not easily developed or cultivated. It is closely associated with the Aristotelian virtues and a willingness to live in a certain way no matter what the external consequences may be. A 'good' human being shows integrity in all their actions and values this above everything else. Robert Mueller (the former director of the FBI, decorated US Marine who served in Vietnam and special prosecutor into allegations of Russian intervention in the US elections) said in an address at a Massachusetts boarding school:

> You can be smart, aggressive, articulate and indeed persuasive, but if you are not honest, your reputation will suffer, and once lost a good reputation can never, ever, be regained...
>
> As the saying goes, if you have integrity nothing else matters, and if you do not have integrity, nothing else matters.

Living in the truth is more important that knowing the truth. This may be found in those who are simple and unlearned more than the clever and supposedly intelligent. Where it is unlikely to be found is in the religious fundamentalists who are so sure of their possession of the truth. Not only have such people not done any really serious philosophic thinking, not only are their claims based on the thinnest of grounds but more than this they are dangerous. As the Spanish philosopher Unamuno puts it:

Those who believe they believe in God
But without passion in their hearts
Without anguish of mind,
Without uncertainty,
Without doubt,
Even at times without despair
Believe only in the idea of God
Not in God himself.

Galileo Galilei in *The Assayer* 1619 ("The experimental method and dependence on received wisdom") dealt with the issue of whom one should listen to when considering complex questions:

Witnesses are examined in doubtful matters which are past and transient not in those which are actual and present. A judge must seek by means of witnesses to determine whether Pietro injured Giovanni last night but not whether Giovanni was injured since the Judge can see that for himself. But even in conclusions that can be known by means of reason, I say that the testimony of many is not of more value than that of few since the number of people who reason well in complicated matters is much smaller than that of those who reason badly. If reasoning were like hauling that I should agree that several reasoners would be worth more than one since several horses can haul more sacks of grain than one. But reasoning is like racing and not like hauling and a single Barberry steed can outrun a hundred dray horses.

The wise, compassionate, gentle, humble and good person needs to be attended to – these are the Barberry steeds whose lives have been devoted to a search for wisdom and their judgement is of more value than the post-truth herd. Philosophy has become an academic discipline but for the Greeks it was intimately connected with how life should be lived. Someone who called themselves a philosopher but did not reflect the search for wisdom by living a good life would be a contradiction in terms. Today much modern philosophy misses the point of the discipline.

Mystics down the ages have claimed to have seen and dimly understood a greater reality:

> The mystics are convinced that their communion with God is an authentic experience… If a dozen honest men tell me that they have climbed the Matterhorn, it is reasonable to believe that the summit of that mountain is accessible, although I am not likely to get there myself.
> (Dean WR Inge, quoted in Susan Howatch's *Glamorous Powers*)

> The mystical experience seems to those who have it to transport them out of time and space and separate individuality. This, of course, brings us at once among the most formidable philosophical problems. Those mystics who are also philosophers generally hold that neither space nor time is ultimately real.
> (Dean WR Inge, quoted in Susan Howatch's *Glamorous Powers*, "Lay thoughts of a Dean")

> If we believe that the world of time and space, which necessarily supplies the forms under which we picture reality, and the language in which we express our thoughts, is an image or reflection of the real or spiritual world, we must recognise that, except when we are concerned with

absolute values, and even then when we try to interpret them to ourselves, we cannot dispense with religion.
(Dean WR Inge, *Mysticism in Religion*)

The mystics of the great world religions have seen the universe from a different place – they have apprehended a broader view of the nature of reality. Religion at its best has always pointed towards this but, sadly, the religious voice has become debased in the modern world: That does not mean that the potential to seek the Eternal is not present with different religious groups. Bernard Hoose was a Carmelite, head of a major refugee centre in Rome, before becoming a senior lecturer in Ethics at the University of London, but after retiring from lecturing he lost interest in ethics and became more interested in spirituality and mysticism – drawing on the great influences of the Carmelite tradition. In his book *Mysterious God* (Columba Press, 2014) he emphasises the ultimate Mystery that the word 'god' points towards and how easy it is for the word to become a construct that suits human interests:

A glance at the history of the Church reveals to us... that the damaging images of God proved to be problematic... We need only think of God... has so often been presented as an enthusiast for war, a supporter of religious intolerance and a condemning judge who is willing to punish severely even very slight misdemeanors. Small wonder, then, that so many in our time turn their backs on religion. (p. 29/30)

... a notable consequence of bad religion and the misleading ideas of God that it has promoted is that many of the words associated with religious practice (Christian or otherwise) have become decidedly unattractive to many people. (p. 37)

'The Eternal' avoids the problems that have come to be associated with the word 'god' whilst maintaining many of the same values. A sub-theme running through this book has been the issue of potentiality. The potential to form helium and hydrogen, then to form stars and in the nuclear fires of stars to form carbon and so, eventually, life was all present in the singularity (p. 119). The singularity was the reverse of randomness – it was a cosmic seed which included all the vast potential of the universe. Every eventual plant and animal has its own potential. A slug cannot become a seagull, an oak tree cannot become a frog. Human beings, similarly, share potentialities because of what they are as human beings. An absolutely central issue is what it means to fulfil human potential – this is the basis for the Natural Law approach to ethics. Everyone, atheist, agnostic or religious believer, must agree about the existence of potential – where they disagree is as to what this human potential is. Clearly it includes to grow, to learn, to reproduce, to play and appreciate music and art, to work, to run, jump and swim and all the vast range of human potentialities. It does not include the potential to fly unaided, to swim underwater for long periods without breathing aids or to run a sub one-minute mile. Atheists, agnostics and humanists can agree that human beings have the capacity or potentiality for compassion, integrity and acting justly. Where they will disagree is whether these are reflections of Eternal values which give meaning, purpose and hope to human existence or are merely human constructs in a universe devoid of meaning. Additionally, of course, they may disagree as to whether human potentiality includes non-determined freedom and the ability to survive death and, if it does, whether this potentiality can only be understood if these are taken into account.

Potentiality is, therefore, closely related to questions of meaning and purpose. If a transcendent dimension does exist then it provides a framework which distinguishes human beings from animals and, indeed, from artificial intelligence. This has considerable implications for parenting and for education. As previously outlined (p. 193) education in much of the Western world is dedicated to economic success and material prosperity. The wider vision of what it means to be human which the Eternal stands for is often ignored in the face of pressure to achieve examination-related performance which is, rightly, considered the key to success as the world measures the term. This dominant focus all too often marginalises the Arts, music, drama, literature, poetry, philosophy and religious education which can open doors to a wider apprehension of Eternal values and reality. It is in these disciplines that creativity is to be found and enabled to flourish. It takes great courage, however, for a school principal to stand fast for these broader values in the face of governmental, societal and parental pressure.

So where is the Eternal to be found? Not in anything external. Almost everyone who has ever attempted to answer this question sees the answer lying to a large extent on an inner journey – and few people are willing to explore this route. The Islamic poet Jalaluddin Rumi (1207–1273) said the following:

> I searched for God among the Christians and on the Cross and therein I found Him not.
>
> I went into the ancient temples of idolatry; no trace of Him was there.
>
> I entered the mountain cave of Hira and then went as far as Qandhar but God I found not.
>
> With set purpose I fared to the summit of Mount Caucasus and found there only 'anqa's habitation.
>
> Then I directed my search to the Kaaba, the resort of old and young; God was not there even.
>
> Turning to philosophy I inquired about him from Ibn Sina but found Him not within his range.
>
> I fared then to the scene of the Prophet's experience of a great divine manifestation only a "two bow-lengths' distance from him" but God was not there even in that exalted court.

Finally, I looked into my own heart and there I saw Him;
He was nowhere else.
(Translated by Coleman Barks)

If there is something Eternal in human beings, then it will not be
found by scientific experiment or, indeed, by rational enquiry.
It will be found in beauty, in creativity, in nature, in stillness
and silence and sometimes in certain forms of music. It will be
found in lives of compassion, empathy, mercy, kindness and
forgiveness. Pointers to it can be found in the great mystics
from all the world's major religious traditions, but reading their
writings is not the same as a personal search for it. One cannot
learn to swim by reading books about swimming or even by
lying on the floor and practising arm and leg movements. It is a
necessary requirement of learning to swim that one has to enter
the water and to embark on the training necessary: So it is with
the search for the Eternal.

Henry David Thoreau went to live very simply in the woods
because he found there a wisdom which could not be found
amongst his busy friends and acquaintances who had not
thought deeply about life. He said:

I do believe in simplicity. It is astonishing as well as sad, how
many trivial affairs even the wisest thinks he must attend to
in a day; how singular an affair he thinks he must omit. When
the mathematician would solve a difficult problem, he first
frees the equation of all incumbrances, and reduces it to its
simplest terms. So simplify the problem of life, distinguish
the necessary and the real. Probe the earth to see where your
main roots run.

I went to the woods because I wished to live deliberately, to
front only the essential facts of life, and see if I could not learn
what it had to teach, and not, when I came to die, discover

that I had not lived.
(Letter to Harrison Blake, March 27, 1848)

Thoreau also said that most people live lives of quiet desperation – and this is precisely because they have been occupied with 'busyness', with work, buying things, conforming to the expectation of others. The Eternal challenges the generally accepted assumptions and that is why it is so hard to bring people to recognise its importance. Work is, of course, needed but only for the essentials – most of the 'stuff' with which people surround themselves and which they see as 'necessary' are mere distractions.

The first step in seeking the Eternal is to take time to become an individual, to be willing to spend time in silence – ideally amidst the natural world. But this is not the same as just sitting in a room and being quiet or even going for a walk with the dog. Being still, meditation or mindfulness as some call it, requires a personal focus. It requires a person to start on the journey to controlling their mind. To some this may seem odd, but the mind of most people is a riot of confusion, jumping from one thought to another, stimulated by the outer environment. In the animated film *Inside Out*, a series of characters represent the different emotions that vie for the control of a young girl and her parents. Anger, Joy, Sadness, Disgust, and Fear each dominate at different times and can easily be influenced by outside events. What the film fails to address is who or what controls these emotions. For most people, the answer is either 'nothing' as the emotions rule or else they are controlled by outside events. Kant recognised the dangers of this and argued that being human was grounded in the necessity for emotions and instincts to be controlled by reason, but this is not easily done. Animals are dominated by instinct – they do not rationally reflect on their behaviour. It is the ability to use reason that distinguishes human beings from animals. There is nevertheless a sense of an almost infinite regress within a person: The emotions have to be controlled by reason, reason needs to be controlled by the mind and one's 'self' needs to control the mind. But what is this 'self'? It is this 'self' that talk of dualism is intended to affirm but few today hold to the idea of a disembodied 'something' – instead the 'self' is something that needs to be developed and created. Being a self, being an individual is not automatic. It requires commitment and dedication.

Kant's emphasis on rationality alone is mistaken – if rationality is the key ingredient then this can stifle creativity and innovation. Creativity, origination and challenges to the status quo and to accepted wisdom do not spring from rationality alone. Many of the greatest artists have lived their commitment to creativity to the exclusion of all else and, as a result, have died in poverty but they have been driven by a different set of priorities and a recognition of the pearl of great price, something of greater value than material success and recognition.

Becoming an individual means embarking on the exceptionally hard process of taking control of oneself. This is the essence of Buddhist and Hindu teaching as it is of the practice of Yoga and, indeed, the modern exercise of mindfulness. Only someone who has achieved at least some control of their own mind can be a person who has some control over themselves and can, thereby, start on the journey to becoming an individual. Some, of course, will regard this idea as absurd and will argue that every human being is an individual simply by being alive – but this is a mistake. As we have seen (p. 88) human freedom is massively constrained and formed by cultural, media, nurture and genetic influences. Freedom, this book has argued, is an achievement and it is hard won. It is only possible to be free if one is in control of one's own mind, and this is a first and necessary requirement for any understanding of the Eternal. To say it is a 'necessary' requirement is not, however, to say that it is sufficient and it is also essential to come to recognise the transience of the temporal world and to be willing to look beneath this transience.

'Living in the light of eternity' is to see the unity of all things as well as the order and purpose that underpins all reality. Einstein said:

> A human being is a part of a whole, called by us universe, a part limited in time and space. He experiences himself, his thoughts and feelings as something separated from the rest… a kind of optical delusion of his consciousness. This delusion is a kind of prison for us, restricting us to our personal desires and to affection for a few persons nearest to us. Our task must be to free ourselves from this prison by widening our circle of compassion to embrace all living creatures and the whole of nature in its beauty. Nobody is able to achieve this completely but striving for such achievement is, in itself, a part of the liberation and a foundation for inner security.
> (Letter dated February 12, 1950, quoted in *The New York Times*, March 1972)

This is what the Japanese call "seeing things sono-mama" in their unity, which in William Blake's terms is to: "hold infinity in the palm of your hand, and eternity is an hour." Tennyson made the same point in his poem "Flower in the Crannied Wall":

> Flower in the crannied wall,
> I pluck you out of the crannies,
> I hold you here, root and all, in my hand,
> Little flower – but if I could understand
> What you are, root and all, and all in all,
> I should know what God and man is.

A Japanese Haiku poet of the eighteenth century, Bashō produced the following:

When closely inspected,
One notices a nazuna in bloom
Under the hedge.

The nazuna is a tiny wildflower which is hardly noticeable, but it beautifully fulfils its purpose. The difference between Tennyson, the Western poet, and Bashō is significant – the one plucks the flower whilst the other leaves it be and contemplates its beauty. Both, however, reflect what Plato had in mind when he sees time as a necessary limitation and eternity as existing beyond time and space yet intimately connected to the temporal realm. Time and eternity are inseparable, but time will not be understood without coming to see the connection. To see the temporal realm as the only reality is to only see the world of appearance. The majority, the herd, who can only see appearance, are locked into a cave of ignorance both about the meaning and purpose of existence and about the nature of reality itself. Time is, as Plato says, "the moving image of eternity". Spinoza expressed this by talking of seeing the world "sub specie aeternitatis" (under the aspect of eternity). Spinoza's "eternal" perspective is reflected in his *Ethics* (Part V, Prop. XXIII, Scholium), where he seeks to arrive at an ethical theory that is eternally valid and absolute. It is a call to see the world in a different perspective – yet not just another alternative view of reality but an absolute view, as if 'from above'.

Reality is fundamentally mysterious – in some ways it is incredible that any serious scientist can pass through a doorway since she or he knows that the doorway, the floor on which they are standing and their own bodies are in fact ultimately not composed of matter but of potential electrons and that most of what we take to be matter is, in fact, empty space. The floor on which we stand is ethereal, 'unreal' – will we not fall through it? The serious scientist should be deeply perturbed. We accept that we will not fall through the floor but this is not a conclusion arrived at by science but by trust in the nature of the universe which we can only dimly comprehend. Heisenberg, Bohr, Born and others have overthrown the ideas of strict causality. Consciousness defies explanation or analysis except in behaviourist terms which reduces human beings to being no more than a complex machine developed by the random process of natural selection. It is, indeed, easier for a camel to pass through the eye of a needle than for a strict verificationist to walk through a door. The insistence of empirical science as the only way of comprehending reality is simply too limited. Consciousness (which we do not begin to understand) can give us access to a broader view of what reality is that testing cannot arrive at.

Carl Jung, in *Memories, Dreams, Reflections*, wrote:

What we are to our inward vision, and what man appears to be sub specie aeternitatis, can only be expressed by way of myth.

Myths can convey truth, they can lead us to see the world in a different way and therefore challenge our normal way of thinking. Myths challenge conventional thinking, they call us out beyond the prison of the verificationist's and materialist's cave, they seek to show us (and we may not see their message) that reality is far more complex than we can imagine and that our trivial pursuits are mere distractions from the main purpose of existence. They call us beyond single and twofold vision to Blake's fourfold vision.

Martin Luther King Jr. (1929–1968) said:

Cowardice asks the question – is it safe?
Expediency asks the question – is it politic?
Vanity asks the question – is it popular?

But conscience asks the question – is it right?
And there comes a time when one must take a position
that is neither safe, nor politic, nor popular;
but one must take it because it is right.

Seeing the world sub specie aeternitatis is to see that questions
of safety, political expediency, popularity or other worldly ways
of looking at things are mistaken because there is Truth, there
is Justice, there is Integrity, there is Meaning, there is Mercy,
there is Love and these are worth standing for, sacrificing for
and if necessary dying for. These are, also, the only things
worth living for – they are built into the very structure of the
universe and any human life devoted to anything else will end
in disappointment, despair and disillusion. To be sure, most of
us seek to distract ourselves through shopping, relationships,
career, sex, money, sport, hobbies or other activities, but
when we come to die all these will be seen to have been empty
pastimes. Human beings seek to distance themselves from the
reality of life, they take refuge in these distractions as a way of
avoiding confronting reality. This is recognised by all the great
religions. For instance:

Taking refuge is the first step on the Buddhist path to
inner freedom, but it is not something new. We have been
taking refuge all our lives, though mainly in external
things, hoping to find security and happiness. Some of us
take refuge in money, some in drugs. Some take refuge in
food, in mountain-climbing or in sunny beaches. Most of us
seek security and satisfaction in a relationship with a man
or a woman. Throughout our lives we have drifted from
one situation to the next, always in the expectation of final
satisfaction. Our successive involvements may sometimes
offer temporary relief but, in sober truth, seeking refuge in
physical possessions and transient pleasures merely deepens

our confusion rather than ending it.
(Shunryu Suzuki, *Zen Mind, Beginner's Mind*, Weatherhill, 1982, p. 7)

So how can an Eternal dimension be recognised? How can the world be seen in a different way? The first step, as set out above, is to be in control of oneself and that means controlling one's mind – but this is only the first step. This is essential as it is the beginning of ceasing to be a member of the herd, moved this way and that by innumerable unforeseen pressures. If one sees a flock of birds wheeling round and constantly changing direction, then this is a good picture of the sort of lives most people lead. To challenge and question one's peers, upbringing and culture one must begin to alter one's perspective, for instance by developing a feeling of reverence for the natural world, of wonderment at its beauty and at the forces that brought it into being. This is what Kant meant when he talked of aesthetics making a demand on us. It is what Marcel found in the beauty of the Hawthorn blossom in Proust's "Swann's Way". It is what Etty Hillesum found in the Westerbork transit camp (where she was held before being executed in Auschwitz): When looking at the beauty of the Jasmine flowers in the camp she came to recognise meaning and purpose in the universe in spite of seeing, every day, the grim, dehumanised faces of the Nazi guards. It is this recognition of beauty that underpins Franciscan theology in the Christian tradition. More than any other type of theology, the Franciscans focus on simplicity, love and, above all, beauty as pointing toward the transcendent. In Islam the beauty of mathematics expressed in tessellation produces complex and intricate patterns, and can lead the mind towards the Eternal and away from day to day realities.

Some will, of course, simply reject the call of the Eternal and will say that, for instance, beauty and justice are entirely human creations which lie solely in the eye of the beholder. Once again there is no proof that a transcendent, Eternal reality exists: All anyone can do is to be willing to be open to this possibility whilst recognising that appreciation of its existence may not arrive. A person cannot will themselves to find beauty – all they can do is to provide time and space to be open to an alternative perspective. There is a sense in which one does not find Truth, Truth finds the individual – but only if they are open to the possibility.

These are preconditions for having any appreciation of the Eternal, but they alone are not enough. They are, as it were, a prelude and there is no guarantee that even if someone were to follow them he or she would necessarily learn to see the world in a different way. An example might be helpful. Imagine someone is visiting New York and agrees to meet a friend at the Museum of Modern Art for coffee at 10.30. Whilst they are waiting they receive a call from the friend who says she has been unavoidably delayed and will be 90 minutes late. It is raining. They may decide to shelter inside the museum and they see some of the exhibits. Many appear strange and quite a few simply ridiculous. The person cannot conceive why anyone would pay a high price for such rubbish. Nevertheless, they reflect that this is one of the finest museums of modern art in the world. They have not studied modern art and they understand that their reaction may simply be ignorance. They can choose to walk out and mentally write off all modern art, or can decide to go on a course to try to understand why many regard the works inside the museum as masterpieces. It is rather like that with Eternity. Some of the greatest minds in history as well as some individuals who have lived the most remarkable lives have been convinced of the existence of a transcendent realm and Eternal values. A person can choose to write them off as stupid, naïve and perhaps psychologically deluded – or they can set out to seek to understand why they have devoted their lives in the way they have.

All the vast complexity of the natural world was built into the potentiality of the singularity 13.7 billion years ago and the wildflower is as much the outworking of this potentiality as are human beings. The process is the reverse of blind chance – affirmation of Eternity is an affirmation of meaning, purpose, creativity, hope, love and order which underlies the whole of reality.

Seeking the Eternal necessarily requires an absence of busyness, a life of simplicity, a rejection of striving for achievement, a reorientation of priorities and a willingness to see beauty in everything and everywhere. It involves recognising that all those things which 'the world' prizes so greatly are in fact meaningless and like children's toys. The true nature of reality will never be found by those who are preoccupied with money, success, power and reputation. Ownership of 'things' gets in the way of simplicity. All great religious traditions have recognised this yet, today, it is a message that is almost universally ignored.

In the 13th century, two Christian religious orders achieved great support in the West – these were the Dominicans and Franciscans. They both preached lives of simplicity and called people to follow the teaching of Jesus of Nazareth. They were dedicated to 'apostolic poverty' emulating Jesus' early disciples in living simply and setting how to show the wisdom that lay beneath it. Yet in 1308 the Catholic Magisterium condemned as a heresy the claim that Jesus and his disciples were poor, and the Dominicans and Franciscans were forced to become incredibly wealthy in the same way as other religious orders and the Church itself. As so often, the message of the founder of a great religion was subverted by those in power. This is still seen today, particularly, in the United States, with what has been called 'prosperity theology' – this claims that wealth and success are due to working hard, worshipping God and giving generously to the Church. Failure and poverty are the reverse. This is a complete betrayal of the Christian message with its commitment to the poor, the weak, the marginalised and the vulnerable.

The great mystics of the diverse traditions have all recognised the importance of solitude, time to be still and to become 'aware'. This is not an easy path to follow. We are so busy, so preoccupied with the myriad activities necessary for survival that the very idea of being still and living simply is alien to us. If the Eternal exists, then it is not to be found only by mystics or those with a particular religious upbringing – it must be a feature of the universe that is in principle accessible to all human beings if they will only be open to it. The Eternal must be a central part of reality and must, in principle, be recognisable by all if they would take the time and effort to allow themselves to be open to it. The rigorous scientist is not asked to abandon any part of his science or his rigour – just to be open to the possibility that the empirical method alone is inadequate to capture the whole of reality. Humans have always been seekers of Truth, but Truth cannot be arrived at by an inventory of facts just as what it means to be human cannot be arrived at by a genetic analysis of the chromosomes from which we are derived.

'The Eternal' may be regarded as a negation of finitude, a negation of the transiency of the world of temporality and an affirmation both of eternal values and of eternal meaning which can be glimpsed beneath the world of appearance. Buddhism is sometimes characterized as a way of negation and, in particular, a negation of the principle of non-contradiction. It seeks to show unity beneath diversity and significance beneath insignificance. The great Buddhist Masters would often talk in riddles which were not capable of being understood except by someone who was genuinely seeking enlightenment. Enlightenment means the acquisition of wisdom, coming (after great striving) to stop desiring, to stop wanting things, to be willing to live in the immediate present which is no different from the past or the future, and to be willing to see beneath the surface and to understand the unity beneath diversity.

In this book, there have been few references to God – and that is because the word God has become devalued and denuded of meaning and content. Jewish rabbis have always recognised the difficulty of speaking about God. Moses Maimonides said that the only thing that can be meaningfully said about God was what God said to Moses when Moses asked for his name – God's reply from the burning bush was, "I am that I am." According to Rabbi Yosef Wineberg, Maimonides stated that, "God is knowledge," and God's Essence, Being and Knowledge are completely identical. Wineberg quotes Maimonides as stating:

This [form of unity] wherein G-d's knowledge and so on is one with G-d Himself is beyond the capacity of the mouth to express, beyond the capacity of the ear to hear, and beyond the capacity of the heart of man to apprehend clearly.
(*Shaar Hayichud Vehaemunah*, Ch. 8)

Negative theology has an important place in the Western Christian tradition. The 9th century theologian John Scotus Erigena wrote:

We do not know what God is. God Himself does not know what He is because He is not anything [i.e., "not any created thing"]. Literally God is not, because He transcends being.

When Scotus says that, "God is not anything" and "God is not", he does not reject God but is emphasising that God cannot be said to exist in the way that creation exists. He is using apophatic language to emphasise that God is "other". Theologians like Meister Eckhart and St John of the Cross show similar tendencies towards the apophatic tradition in the West. In *The Cloud of Unknowing* and *The Dark Night of the Soul* these are particularly a focus. St Thomas Aquinas was probably the greatest Christian philosopher of the last two thousand years, yet all his writings serve but to affirm that unknowability of God. Both Rudolf Otto and Karl Barth refer to God as "wholly other" whilst the Jesuit theologian Karl Rahner describes God as, "Holy Mystery". Anthony de Mello says, "Every word, every image used for God is a distortion more than a description." For religious people, language may be used of God, but the content is so severely limited that it is better to remain silent. To speak of 'The Eternal' can be a way of seeking to recapture in our own times that which previous generations have designated God.

Religious people talk of 'God' but every serious theologian will accept that it is very far from clear what this word means. The Jewish writer, Martin Buber, was staying on a great German estate in 1932 and had got up early to read the proofs of a book. He met a "noble old thinker", as Buber described him, already up before him, and at this thinker's request read the proofs aloud. When Buber was finished, the old man said with great vehemence:

How can you bring yourself to say "God" time after time? How can you expect your readers will take the word in the sense in which you wish it to be taken? What you mean by God is something beyond all human grasp and comprehension, but in speaking about it you have lowered it to human conceptualization. What word of all human speech is used misused, so defiled, so desecrated as this! All the innocent blood that has been shed for it has robbed it of its radiance. All the injustices that it has been used to cover has effaced its features. When I hear "God" it sometimes seems blasphemous.

Buber says that he sat silent. Then he felt as if a power from on high had entered into him and what he then replied he says he can only indicate. It was as follows:

Yes, it is the most heavily ladened of all human words. None has become so soiled, so mutilated. Just for this reason I may not abandon it. Generations of men have laid the burden of their anxious lives upon this word and weighed it to the ground; it lies in the dust and bears their whole burden. The races of men with their religious factions have torn the word to pieces; they have killed for it and died for it. And it bears their finger marks and their blood. Where might I find a word like it to describe the highest? If I took the purest, the most sparkling from the treasure chambers of the philosophers I could only capture thereby an unbinding product of thought. I could not capture the presence of Him whom generations of men have honoured and degraded with their awesome living and dying... Certainly they draw caricatures and write "God" underneath; they murder one another and say in "God's" name. But when all madness and delusion fall to dust, when they stand over against Him in the loneliest darkness and no longer say, "He, He", but rather "Thou", shout "Thou", all of them with one word, and when they then add "God", is it not He that they implore, the one living God, the God of the children of man? Is it not He who hears them? ... We must esteem those who interdict it because they rebel against the injustice and wrong which are so often referred to "God" for authorization. But we may not give it up... We cannot cleanse the word "God" and make it whole but, defiled and mutilated as it is, we can raise it from the ground and set it over an hour with great care.

The old man got up, came over to Buber, laid his hand on his shoulder and said, "Come, let us be friends."

The word 'God' is now so defiled, so misunderstood, so misused that perhaps it is not possible to cleanse it from the guilt attributed to it by human beings which is why, perhaps, the word 'Eternal' may be an effective way in today's world at gesturing towards the same underlying reality. It also avoids the mistaken idea that whatever the word 'God' refers to is some sort of anthropomorphic superman figure – no serious theologian or philosopher thinks in these terms but, sadly, the Christian decision in the c 9th century to allow artistic representations of God (generally as an old man with a white beard) has encouraged this absurdity. One of the greatest enemies of the Eternal is the idea of God as some person who rewards and punishes and whose commands are the basis for ethics. This God has been responsible for oppression, wars, corruption, abuse of power and many other evils. Whatever 'God' means it is that which underpins meaning, purpose, order and the fundamental Eternal values that Plato argued for.

Einstein said:

The most beautiful thing we can experience is the mysterious. It is the source of all true art and all science. He to whom this emotion is a stranger, who can no longer pause to wonder and stand rapt in awe, is as good as dead: his eyes are closed.

Meister Eckhart said that, "Theologians may quarrel, but the mystics of the world speak the same language," and it is the Eternal that mystics of the world have sought and often found. For the mystic, the Eternal is real – a friend with whom they live and from who they are never parted. It is both a sure refuge, a place of sanctuary and a terrifying challenge to all the normal preconceptions and preoccupations of life. Above all, it is connected to Truth. Evelyn Underhill said:

In mysticism that love of truth which we saw as the beginning of all philosophy leaves the merely intellectual sphere, and takes on the assured aspect of a personal passion. Where the philosopher guesses and argues, the mystic lives and looks; and speaks, consequently, the disconcerting language of first-hand experience, not the neat dialectic of the schools. Hence whilst the Absolute of the metaphysicians remains a diagram – impersonal and unattainable – the Absolute of the mystics is lovable, attainable, alive.

(*Mysticism: A Study in the Nature and Development of Spiritual Consciousness*)

Seeking the Eternal does demand a personal passion, it does demand going beyond (not against) a purely rational approach. It certainly does not mean a retreat from the world. Living in the Eternal, recognising the demands of Eternity requires engagement with the world but it also needs to be accompanied by times of stillness and silence. The two are mutually intertwined. Eternity pervades the whole of reality but also makes an enduring and continuing demand on us to live according to its values – and these values require a rejection of the normal way of looking at things. Once power, success and reputation no longer matter, then these will no longer be driving forces. This does not mean that they may or may not occur as a secondary effect or by-product, but they cannot be pursued as objectives or purposes. They are hollow, ephemeral and cannot motivate greatness. True greatness does not lie in exterior achievements but in becoming the sort of person who has power – and the power is of a different order to worldly power. First and foremost, as we have seen, it means power over one's self so that one realises who one is and what one is seeking to become. The first step to any search for wisdom is to become a solitary individual who can deal with being alone and be at peace, who can deal with failure and lack of recognition and accept these are trivial, who can accept betrayal in love and a world that rejects beauty, justice and wisdom but still not become cynical or disillusioned. Seeking the Eternal involves creativity, openness to what is new and a willingness to challenge prevailing orthodoxies – it means being 'other' than the world.

Those who relate their lives to the Absolute, The Eternal or what some call God and others living 'sub specie aeternitatis' will stand for values that endure. Wittgenstein described the good life as the world seen sub specie aeternitatis and considered that it is this that unites aesthetics and ethics. These include personal integrity, justice, the rights of those who are weak and vulnerable as well as compassion for everyone. People who live in this way will also show in their lives a fierce engagement with and rejection of those who seek to do or who are manifestations of evil. It was this message with which Dietrich Bonhoeffer engaged and with which he wrestled and which eventually led to his death.

Once someone recognises that death may not be the end and/or once the existence of Eternal values is accepted then everything changes. All the normal priorities of life fade into insignificance and are seen to be worthless and of little account. The pursuit of success, fame, money, sexual gratification or owning things becomes really insignificant once one accepts that human potential lies beyond merely fulfilling animal functions. Someone who recognises this will march to a different drummer and it is this insight (and it is an insight or perhaps, as Albrecht Ritschl described it, a "value judgement") that underpins all the great world religions.

Above all the Eternal provides a recognition of hope – hope in the face of despair and disaster; hope that good will triumph over evil; hope that justice will endure and oppression is only transient; hope that human creativity and the power of love are not an illusion; hope that every human life has meaning and value. It is very difficult to hold on to hope when everything seems dark and life seems devoid of purpose or meaning. Far easier to curse the darkness rather than seeking to light a candle. There will be many who reject hope as a delusion – the world, they will say, is meaningless and full of pain and suffering. Life is devoid of purpose and all endeavour ends in disappointment and disillusion. The only remedy is depression or, perhaps, suicide. They may, of course, be right, but they could also be wrong.

It is through religion, with all its multiple manifestations and many flaws, that Goodness and the Eternal have traditionally manifested themselves. One can easily, and rightly, criticise doctrines, power structures, abusive priests and fallible human beings who claim a religious affiliation and seek to impose their views on others. Nevertheless, beneath this superficial (but nevertheless real) mess lies the enduring message of the Eternal and, sometimes, like a ray of sunlight through a stained-glass window; the tessellation of a mathematical pattern in a mosque; a funeral pyre on the Ganges or the Buddhist monk meditating lies the reality of something that endures. This is the only thing that makes life worth living and when we are forced down into the depths of mud in the post-truth cave it is the only thing worth holding on to, fighting for and, if necessary, dying for.

Affirmation of the Eternal is as relevant as it has ever been and its significance is as enduringly profound. The fact that most people think that its time has passed does not negate its Truth. The more it appears to change the more its essence remains the same. Truth matters. The Eternal matters. In both cases we may never achieve more than an approximation but the search for both are the only things that make human life truly worth living and the only thing that, ultimately, brings satisfaction and peace of mind.

Chapter Thirteen

Postscript

Human beings constantly push the envelope of our understanding of what it means to be human – we constantly amaze ourselves with our intellectual, creative and other abilities. We discover that we are more and more complex than we have previously supposed and our potentialities and consciousness resist definition and the limits that are often imposed on us. We can understand something of the mystery of the universe (and this, in itself, is extraordinary) as well as creating the most sublime music, poetry and art. We are conscious and can contemplate questions such as the meaning and purpose of our existence. We are continually dissatisfied, and this pushes us beyond the narrow confines by which we like to define ourselves. Instead of focussing on understanding just how far human potentialities can be expanded, we instead diminish ourselves and see ourselves simply as biological mechanisms without meaning, purpose or telos. We are like children who are content to remain children instead of being willing to grow to adulthood. The great religions of the world have all called on human beings to recognise their true potentialities but instead of pushing human beings to develop these potentialities, religions increasingly collude with society to make us satisfied with mediocrity and indifference.

The little stream that is Truth resists the power of postmodernism and relativism on the one hand and fundamentalism on the other. It sometimes seems irrelevant to the modern world, is often ignored but is nevertheless persistent and enduring. It will not be eradicated and will suffer the ridicule of the post-truth advocates without itself being changed. It exists in the hearts and minds of those who think deeply and who care about the nature of human beings and the incredibly rich potentiality which we share. It sometimes finds it hard to speak in a world dominated by powerful media voices, yet it knows it will endure long after the latest intellectual fashions have turned to dust. It is grounded in the Eternal and, because of this, cannot be obliterated.

Accepting the existence of Eternal values means rejecting relativism and seeking to live a life of integrity. There are things worth living and dying for, and these do not depend on culture. They are grounded in the virtues but shown in acts of justice, compassion, humility, love and mercy as well as an acceptance that there is hope and meaning beyond the trivia with which most people occupy themselves. Living in this way requires courage and the willingness to question the media, politicians and received wisdom which 'everyone' accepts. It also requires a refusal to go along with the false truths of those who seek only their own ends. It means affirming the claim that Truth Matters.

Naturally there are multiple perspectives and it is right to recognise these, but acceptance of alternative interpretations does not negate the idea of underlying claims to Truth. The voice of the Eternal has been largely silenced and it is necessary and urgent to recapture it. Greatness is directly linked to fulfilling the human potential we all share but which most of us refuse to recognise as, once we do so, we may be forced to respond to the challenge it presents. This book may or may not have been an adequate attempt but at the least it may be that it will prompt others to make a more successful effort. If nothing else, perhaps, it may serve to rekindle interest in the task and to pick up the torch which has too long been trampled in the post-truth dust.

Epilogue

In 1904, Baron von Hügel, a devout Catholic, and Claude Montefiore, a liberal Jewish theologian, brought together a group of Jewish and Christian theologians and thinkers who included the Chief Rabbi and the Archbishop of Canterbury. They were eminent figures of their time and they founded the London Society for the Study of Religions. The Archbishop and Chief Rabbi have been honorary members ever since. The aim of the Society was, however, not quite what the title implied – this was no group merely studying religion. They wanted to do something else. The members came from different branches of Judaism and Christianity and they recognised that their background beliefs were significantly in tension, yet they were convinced that in the old faiths there lay a wisdom which was not found elsewhere and yet which was highly relevant in what was then seen as the 'modern world'. It was a world of Victorian streets, the first motorised taxi cabs, the first cars and aeroplanes and one in which industrialization had transformed society. Fast ships crossed the globe, railways covered the whole of Europe and much of the rest of the world and progress was to be seen everywhere. Yet beneath all these advances, these great thinkers saw that something was increasingly being neglected and that was what they called 'The Eternal'. By this they meant a transcendent order, a transcendent meaning and set of values which could not be explained in normal terms.

The mission statement of the London Society was as follows:

LSSR FOUNDERS STATEMENT 1904
Thoughtful men of widely divergent religious systems are awaking to the fact that the great extension of our modern

knowledge – while in itself so impressive a manifestation of human greatness – threatens to result in a loss of **spiritual insight and power**, on which that greatness itself must ultimately depend.

Through many of the ancient Faiths **a peace of soul** has been reached not easy to possess today, and yet never more needed, both for its own sake and its far-reaching consequences for good.

But, confident in the enduring worth of the ever-widening scope and suggestion of modern thought, we feel that criticism of the old in the light of the new is, for us, at once a supreme act of reverence to the greatness of the past and an essential condition of **spiritual vitality** in the future.

That difference of attitude and tradition must continue to exist among us we fully recognise, but, **where there is approximate unity of aim**, we feel that these should only increase the security and comprehensiveness of study.

It will therefore be the object of this society to include **devout men of every school**, and to welcome all new thought that seeks **to restore or re-state for our own time and in the language of today those revelations and apprehensions of the Eternal** which have in different ages given greatness to the past.

The bold letters are my own but they represent, perhaps, the most significant parts of the statement. The document affirms the existence of "spiritual insight and power" and a "spiritual vitality" that is directly linked to "peace of soul". This was not simply a different way of looking at the contemporary world; it represented a clear affirmation of the importance of the transcendent and the Eternal in a world which was dominated, as ours is today, by ever-increasing knowledge but which could not be expressed simply by this increased knowledge. Indeed the increased knowledge was seen as leading to a loss of this spiritual power. The document also recognises that although there were significant differences between 'schools' (today we might instead refer to 'beliefs systems') nevertheless the greatest thinkers within these systems shared a common, even if approximate, 'unity of aim', and they shared insights into the 'Eternal' which were not found elsewhere. These intimations of the Eternal were, the Founders held, what really provided 'greatness' to the civilisations of the past.

I was invited to join the Society in 1987 (admission is always by invitation only – and the number of members is kept small, never exceeding 30) and was president in 1996 for a two-year term. Some eminent people were members – including major Jewish, Christian, Muslim, Quaker and other thinkers as well as atheists. The original members were originally united by a common search, although there were differences in how this search was to be interpreted. More than one hundred years after the first meeting of the Society, the search on which the original members embarked is more relevant than ever. Nevertheless, I resigned from the Society, with considerable regret, in 2017 as I came to the conclusion that it has lost its way. It was no longer interested in the vision that its founders had set out. Instead it had become a comfortable talking shop, in the highly congenial surroundings of the Athenaeum (one of the most prestigious London clubs) with leather armchairs and excellent wine. Relativism had, in my view, permeated even the Athenaeum's distinguished halls. The papers that continued to be delivered were all related to the theme of religion in some general way, but the idea that they might be in some way part of a search for the Eternal was relegated to the pages of history. The tide of relativism and postmodernism that has come to dominate the modern world had, in my view, sucked the lifeblood out of the Society and I left it with great regret. Nevertheless, the leaving prompted this book.

I am grateful to Wendy Rowe and Moira Siara for reading the mss and for their comments.

PETER VARDY
Bracken Ridge Farm, Yorkshire, England
2018

Index

**IFF
BOOKS**

ACADEMIC AND SPECIALIST

Iff Books publishes non-fiction. It aims to work with authors and
titles that augment our understanding of the human condition,
society and civilisation, and the world or universe in which
we live.
If you have enjoyed this book, why not tell other readers by
posting a review on your preferred book site.

Recent bestsellers from Iff Books are

The Fall
Steve Taylor
The Fall discusses human achievement versus the issues of war,
patriarchy and social inequality.
Paperback: 978-1-90504-720-8 ebook: 978-184694-633-2

Brief Peeks Beyond
Critical Essays on Metaphysics, Neuroscience, Free Will,
Skepticism and Culture
Bernardo Kastrup
An incisive, original, compelling alternative to current mainstream
cultural views and assumptions.
Paperback: 978-1-78535-018-4 ebook: 978-1-78535-019-1

Framespotting
Changing How You Look at Things Changes How You See Them
Laurence & Alison Matthews
A punchy, upbeat guide to framespotting. Spot deceptions and hidden assumptions; swap growth for growing up. See and be free.
Paperback: 978-1-78279-689-3 ebook: 978-1-78279-822-4

Is There an Afterlife?
David Fontana
Is there an Afterlife? If so what is it like? How do Western ideas of the afterlife compare with Eastern? David Fontana presents the historical and contemporary evidence for survival of physical death.
Paperback: 978-1-90381-690-5

Nothing Matters
A Book About Nothing
Ronald Green
Thinking about Nothing opens the world to everything by illuminating new angles to old problems and stimulating new ways of thinking.
Paperback: 978-1-84694-707-0 ebook: 978-1-78099-016-3

Panpsychism
The Philosophy of the Sensuous Cosmos
Peter Ells
Are free will and mind chimeras? This book, anti-materialistic but respecting science, answers: No! Mind is foundational to all existence.
Paperback: 978-1-84694-505-2 ebook: 978-1-78099-018-7

Punk Science
Inside the Mind of God
Manjir Samanta-Laughton
Many have experienced unexplainable phenomena; God, psychic
abilities, extraordinary healing and angelic encounters. Can
cutting-edge science actually explain phenomena
previously thought of as 'paranormal'?
Paperback: 978-1-90504-793-2

Vagabond Spirit of Poetry
Edward Clarke
Spend time with the wisest poets of the modern age and of the
past, and let Edward Clarke remind you of the importance of
poetry in our industrialized world.
Paperback: 978-1-78279-370-0 ebook: 978-1-78279-369-4

Readers of ebooks can buy or view any of these bestsellers by
clicking on the live link in the title. Most titles are published in
paperback and as an ebook. Paperbacks are available in traditional
bookshops. Both print and ebook formats are available online.

Find more titles and sign up to our readers' newsletter at
http://www.johnhuntpublishing.com/non-fiction

Follow us on Facebook at
https://www.facebook.com/JHPNonFiction
and Twitter at
https://twitter.com/JHPNonFiction